Praise for
Sell with Authority

"Authority" sounds like a word a bully would love: It suggests power, prestige, command. But the truth is that "authority" is more about honing and sharing your expertise through speaking, writing, a point of view. The word "author" is embedded right into "authority." Clever, huh?

What Drew and Stephen have done is given you a field guide to being a true authority, and showing you how to connect that to your growing business. Recommend!

Ann Handley, *CCO, MarketingProfs and WSJ bestselling author of Everybody Writes and Content Rules*

Staying relevant for the future is what professional services businesses are struggling to accomplish. For the first time, a book that gives a realistic plan on how to actually create thought leadership that works. Not theoretical prose, but an actual plan to do it along with examples of best practices. Read it today and put it into action next week!

Renae Krause, *Co-Founder of er marketing*

If I was writing a business and strategy book for marketing agencies, it would be *Sell with Authority*. This book is most likely the only thing standing between your agency and oblivion. Save yourself (and your agency) by following this critical guide to agency success.

Joe Pulizzi, *Author, Killing Marketing, Content Inc. and Epic Content Marketing*

Sell with Authority is the definitive guide to future-proof your agency. As competition increases in our industry, Drew and Stephen have a solution that outlines every step and tool you will need to establish an authoritative position. They give you the right questions including the ones that define your point of differentiation, which is the only way to avoid commoditization of your agency. Read this book, roll up your sleeves, and follow this map to a more profitable future.

Sara Steever, *President of Paulsen*

Incredibly useful! This is the ultimate guide to growing an agency with thought leadership and content marketing. A must-read for every agency owner and manager.

Jay Baer, *Founder of Convince & Convert and co-author of Talk Triggers*

I read Drew and Stephen's book, *Sell with Authority*, and my first reaction was, 'yeah... I know.' I wasn't able to stand back and realize that I had spent a decade fumbling over the concepts in this book - doing them, making mistakes, trying more, trying again – before figuring out what really worked for us.

Sell with Authority is brilliant, because now you don't have to make the same mistakes that we did. Ultimately, things worked out great for our little agency (we sold to WPP in 2014, and the agency then went on to become Mirum, now a part of Wunderman Thompson), but how much better could things have been with a book like this? Stop fumbling around! The agency business has never been more complex. Let Drew and Stephen break it all down for you. I wish I had this book in 2003.

Mitch Joel, *Author, Six Pixels of Separation, Former President of Twist Image/Mirum*

The world around us is changing so fast, it's hard for agency owners – in fact any business owner – to keep up. Selling with Authority is an easy-to-read playbook that explains why these changes are taking place and offers specifics on how we can quickly take action to get in front of the competition.

Stephen Fry, *President of Spindustry*

Want to grow faster? *Sell with Authority* is a must read - an innovative business development framework for agencies of all sizes. Read it. Do it. Sell with authority!

Robin Boehler, *Mercer Island Group*

You're selling the wrong stuff! Don't worry, almost every other agency out there is as well. It's time to stop. Drew and Stephen, in their new book *Sell with Authority* not only tell you what you're selling is wrong, but why it's wrong. You need to be selling gray matter – your thinking and expertise. You need to be an authority. But how do you do that? How do you pivot and make the shift from selling stuff to selling smarts? How do you carve out a position of authority for yourself and your business?

As an agency owner, I can tell you it's not easy. It takes focus and dedication and it's a shift we're continuing to navigate. Drew and Stephen share real-world examples and provide tips, tricks, and tools to get it done. You won't find two individuals more passionate about our profession and more caring about helping you succeed. Do yourself a favor...read this book.

Brad Gillum, *CEO of Willow Marketing*

Sell with
AUTHORITY

Sell with
AUTHORITY

Your Agency's Road Map to Defining It,
Earning It, and Monetizing It

By Drew McLellan & Stephen Woessner

Published in Des Moines, Iowa, by:

Bookpress Publishing
P.O. Box 71532
Des Moines, IA 50325
www.BookpressPublishing.com

Publisher's Cataloging-in-Publication Data

Names: McLellan, Drew M., author. | Woessner, Stephen, 1972-, author.
Title: Sell with authority : your agency's road map to defining it , earning it , and monetizing it / By Drew McLellan & Stephen Woessner.
Description: Des Moines, IA: Bookpress Publishing, 2020.
Identifiers: LCCN 2019917484 | ISBN 978-1-947305-07-6
Subjects: LCSH Selling. | Sales management. | Sales personnel. | Success in business. | BISAC BUSINESS & ECONOMICS / Sales & Selling / General
Classification: LCC HF5438.25 .M3953 2020 | DDC 658.85--dc23

First Edition
Printed in the United States of America
10 9 8 7 6 5 4 3 2 1

Dedications:

It's an amazing gift to grow up with parents who genuinely believe you are capable of anything if you do the work. Ron and Dora McLellan paved the way for any modicum of success I've had and I dedicate this book to their memories. Every day I just try to make them proud.

To Elaine Bacopoulos — it's an honor to be your nephew. You've always been there for me...for all of us. You've shown what it means to be a great parent and demonstrated how to love unconditionally. Your strength is a powerful inspiration to everyone around you, Aunt Elaine — THANK YOU! We love you so very much.

Acknowledgements

We pretty much did this all by ourselves and no one helped.

Okay, maybe we had a little help.

First, if it wasn't weird to write, we'd thank each other. Co-authoring a book is risky business. Will your ideas mesh? Will egos clash? Will the other one bomb the deadline deliverables? Will this project damage our professional relationship or our friendship?

The good news is—none of those things happened. Working together brought out the best in each of us and the book is far better for the collaboration.

When you decide to write a book, it's pretty exhilarating. The idea of sharing what you know and helping others is very appealing. And then you start to actually write it and the exhilaration turns into super late nights (Drew) or 4am alarms (Stephen) and begging forgiveness from family members who haven't seen you emerge from your office in days.

We are grateful for their understanding and patience. We have promised to take them to Denny's for a Grand Slam breakfast with the proceeds of the book.

Our co-workers also deserve a trip to Denny's. There were many days when we were either unavailable because of the book or just grumpy and we blamed it on the book. They kindly looked the other way until we put on our happy faces!

We partnered with Bookpress Publishing to bring our book to life and get it on the bookshelves. Their guidance, advice, and tough questions definitely improved the final result and kept us on track.

We knew we could count on Robin Blake for our cover design and book layout. She's been knocking it out of the park for MMG, AMI, and Predictive ROI for years!

Our final thanks goes to the agencies we work with every day. You are a gift and it's such a privilege to be of service to you. Your courage, your commitment to your teams and clients, and your willingness to step out of your comfort zone is inspiring. Thank you for letting us come along for the ride. This book is our way of saying thanks.

Drew & Stephen

Introduction 1

Chapter One: How Did We Get Here? *(Drew)* 5

Chapter Two: Three Essentials to
Becoming an Authority *(Drew)* 15

Chapter Three: Go Narrow to Monetize *(Stephen)* 27

Chapter Four: Defining Your Point of View *(Drew)* 34

Chapter Five: Be More Than a One-Trick Pony *(Stephen)* 44

Chapter Six: Creating Cornerstone Content *(Drew)* 50

Chapter Seven: The Pros and Cons of Talking *(Drew)* 60

Chapter Eight: Writing as the Hub of
Your Cornerstone Content *(Stephen)* 79

Chapter Nine: Extending your Reach and ROI *(Stephen)* 89

Chapter Ten: Your New Business Blueprint *(Drew)* 97

Chapter Eleven: Build an Audience from Scratch *(Stephen)* 109

Chapter Twelve: How to Monetize Your Content *(Stephen)* 117

Chapter Thirteen: Yes, You Can Get it All Done! *(Stephen)* 128

Chapter Fourteen: Agencies Doing it Well *(Drew)* 136

Chapter Fifteen: The Big Close *(Drew)* 151

Appendix A: Slice and Dice Recipes 155

Appendix B: Tools for Getting it Done 166

Introduction

I want agency owners to win. I particularly want small to mid-size agency owners to win because they are some of the most tenacious, passionate professionals I know. It's why Agency Management Institute (AMI) exists. We do everything in our power to help agency owners gain an unfair advantage. And that's why this book is so important to both me and Stephen.

I believe, and I know Stephen concurs, that this is the future of agencies. This is the way you differentiate yourself. This is how you survive the 99 Design commoditization of the work you've loved doing for decades. This is how we continue to have the privilege of walking alongside our clients as their greatest asset.

We've written this book to be 10 percent philosophy (or theory) and 90 percent actionable lessons and examples, and hopefully an occasional boot on your behind to get going. Today, there are very few agencies who genuinely deliver on what we're teaching. You can have that unfair advantage if you get going now. Seize it.

In writing this book, our goals are clearly defined. We want to help agency owners like you:

- identify your distinct point of view, which creates differentiation for your agency and the ability to charge a premium price.

- create and distribute strategic cornerstone content to your audience to cement your point of view and earn a true position of authority.

- monetize your content marketing efforts so they become a revenue stream rather than an expense.

- replicate and package the process so you can sell it to your prospects and clients.

The "why" was equally clear for us. We believe this is the future of marketing your agency, and the early adoption of this strategy will keep you competitive for years to come. We want you to be one of these early adopters.

In fact, we agree with Joe Pulizzi and Robert Rose when they say in their 2017 book, *Killing Marketing*, that the future of marketing is turning what has historically been a massive expense for businesses into something that can actually become a revenue stream. Imagine if your work generated enough money to cover your fees, and then some. What client wouldn't renew that contract?

Have you ever read one of those books that tells two stories or takes two different points of view, and about halfway through the book, you have to flip it over to read the other half? That's sort of what we're aiming for, but without the flipping.

Most of our focus will be on how agencies can create cornerstone content that not only differentiates them from their competitors, but also generates revenue through a variety of sources. But we also believe that the agencies that master this strategy can leverage it for their clients, too.

Ultimately, this is about growing a thriving, profitable agency that can weather the constant change that seems to be our world's reality. How do you future-proof your shop? How do you actually attract your sweet-spot clients so they're proactively asking you to them? How do you step away from the sea of other agencies so you stand out?

We're going to make the case that ours is the wisest course of action for agency owners seeking to future-proof their agency, but the lion's share of the book is devoted to actually making it happen.

I've been doing this for 30 years now, and back when I was still wet behind the ears professionally speaking, we didn't talk about content. We certainly created it, but we didn't use that term or discuss it much.

We're at the beginning of a huge shift in terms of what agencies provide their clients, and if we take advantage of this opportunity, we can return to the C-suite with our clients. One of the most common complaints I hear from agency owners is, "I'm tired of being treated like a vendor. We used to be a strategic partner. We used to be in the C-suite, and I want to get back to that table."

So let's get you back where you belong.

Drew McLellan

Chapter One:
How Did We Get Here?

(Drew)

Content. When did that become a thing? Stephen and I have both been in the business for more than 25 years, and back when we started our careers, no one was talking about content. But that doesn't mean we weren't creating it.

The industry has evolved a great deal since the first agency over-serviced their client in about 1800 (given the chaos of advertising in the early days, no one has been able to pinpoint precisely when it became a paid profession). One thing has been a constant—since day one, we've helped our clients capture and tell their stories in a way that makes an impact.

Back in the golden days of advertising, agencies were boldly creating content that makes what most agencies do today look rather elementary. In many ways, this new era of what agencies can and should be bringing to their clients (and doing for their own agencies) is taking our industry back to its roots.

Let's look at the trajectory of advertising since the *Mad Men* days. Back then, agencies gave away everything they created in exchange for media commissions. That's how they made their money. Remember, the landscape looked very different. Today, the vast majority of agencies are privately owned, independent, local, and regional, but a century ago, the world of advertising was comprised of large corporate agencies primarily based in New York, L.A., or London. Although they weren't being paid directly for the strategy or creative they produced, those agencies were creating content. Big, bold, culture-changing content. Often, they were also creating an audience from scratch because they needed placement opportunities for their clients.

In some ways, the freedom of not having to worry about how much a tactic would cost or how much time it would take created bigger thinking and fewer boundaries.

Benton & Bowles was an agency based in New York that was launched in 1929 by William Benton and Chester Bowles. They actually invented the radio soap opera so they could create sponsorships and ad placements for their clients who wanted to target homemakers with their message. By 1936, they were responsible for three of the four most popular radio shows on the air, including *As the World Turns*. When television arrived, Benton & Bowles replicated their radio success and launched a TV version of this, their most popular show, in 1956 for their client Proctor & Gamble. P&G sponsored or advertised on that show until it was canceled in 2010. Somewhere along the way, the network bought the show from Benton & Bowles, but they negotiated

P&G's exclusivity as part of the deal.

Even back then, agencies understood that no one sought out advertising. But if you gave them something they valued, they'd gladly accept the advertising as part of the package. This concept of storytelling was part of the agency's DNA, and many of the agency alumni went on to build on that foundation. Shepherd Mead started at B&B as a mail room clerk and worked his way up to Vice President of the company. On his weekends, he wrote the book *How to Succeed in Business Without Really Trying*, which would later be turned into a Broadway hit. Dick Wolf, the creator of the *Law and Order* television series, also got his start at Benton & Bowles.

When we talk about memorable ad campaigns, most of them came from this era. They were filled with memorable characters (the Marlboro Man, Mr. Whipple, and the Jolly Green Giant) and earworm jingles (Wrigley's Doublemint gum, Kellogg's Rice Krispies, and Chevrolet General Motors), and they used these elements to get the audience to connect with the stories and products they were pitching.

Somehow, that sense of storytelling with just a smattering of advertising got watered down between the mid-80s and the early 90s. By then, agencies were no longer surviving on commissions alone. We were being paid piecemeal, like a retail store. This was the start of the laundry list of deliverables tied to agency hours. Clients were beginning to pay for creative execution, markups, and in sporadic cases, strategy.

For most agency owners working today, this is when we got our start. It's the model we grew up on, but it's also the model that began to commoditize what we do. It moved us from dealing with business owners and CEOs and put us on the slippery slope toward procurement and the considerations of agencies as vendors as opposed to business advisors or partners.

On the public relations side of things, it was a little different. Back in the 20th century, PR was really about pitching stories to the media. There was always an element of crisis communication in the mix and some event creation and management, but all in all, it was primarily about influencing the stories that other people told about their clients.

We crossed into the 21st century, and the Internet became more accessible and more commercialized. We began building rudimentary websites along with our traditional creative. Most agencies are still giving away their ideas to get clients to sign off on the list of deliverables, but it's getting a little tougher to make money on media commissions and markups. At this stage, agencies have become doers rather than strategic thinkers, but because we had the skills, software, and media connections, we were still able to charge a premium for our services.

PR agencies continued to tell and shape their clients' stories, but now they didn't have to rely on others alone. They had the first digital version of owned media.

Very few clients had the appetite to invest in developers at the dawn of the Internet age. It was way beyond their comprehension, so agencies enjoyed a very profitable window of time because we knew something the client didn't know and didn't want to learn.

Our world changed when being findable online became a thing. Suddenly the brochureware websites we'd been creating weren't the sum total of what was possible when it came to creating a digital presence. Google, Yahoo, and other early search engines started to hold us accountable for the words on those websites and their relevance to audiences' queries.

One of the most beautiful benefits of the digital emergence is that agencies suddenly found it a little easier to sell ideas and strategies.

The channels were so new that clients depended on their agencies to help them figure out how best to use them. We brought value to every conversation, and we were educating our clients in every meeting. That's a dominant position to be in, as we will discuss throughout this book. Being the teacher who is not only smart, but also willing to share those smarts, is a hard-to-beat strategic position.

This shift also re-ignited the idea of creating content, but in this iteration, content that was helpful and search-engine-optimization (SEO) friendly. At first, we started SEO practices just to please the Google Gods and land our clients on page one, but we quickly discovered that consistent content creation encouraged community growth, referrals, and connections that eventually rang the proverbial cash register.

Google Adwords, the emergence of social media, and digital ads added a complexity to agency work that kept advertisers flush. We were able to merchandise the need to have a digital presence and help clients dip their toes in that water. This was also the time when the phrase "content marketing" was coined by Content Marketing Institute's founder, Joe Pulizzi. The work being done was still pretty basic, but clients and agencies discovered the power of the overall strategy, and suddenly everyone was talking about it, recommending it, and selling it.

And then the recession hit. It was brutal, beating up agencies in a variety of ways. Budgets were slashed, and many agencies were deeply discounting their work just to survive. As clients cut back their budgets and by necessity took some of that work in-house, they got more comfortable developing marketing strategies they'd previously been paying agencies to do.

As the recession ended, the agencies that survived found that the landscape had dramatically changed yet again. The world had become more comfortable with all things digital. The mystique of the Internet had faded, and it was more mainstream, which meant agencies had a tougher time charging a premium for some deliverables.

On top of that, clients had been bootstrapping during the recession and had come out of the recession believing that it was possible to bring some of the work in-house or hire individual freelancers to develop some of the deliverables that they'd previously been paying agencies to do. Even more challenging, the Internet had created a DIY smörgåsbord of tools. Clients could upload and distribute their own media releases, hire a graphic designer, or create a basic website, infographic, or social media post.

Suddenly, the type of work we'd built our agencies on had been commoditized. Even if we earned the opportunity to do the work, we'd trained the clients during the recession that we would work for a marginalized price. Once you lower your prices, it's pretty tough to raise them again, even when the economy bounces back. Our world was picking up the pace, and there was always some "new thing" emerging, whether it was mobile, ads on Instagram, or Tik Tok. We could temporarily charge a premium for a period of time, but as the latest new thing became more the norm, our ability to be the only expert in the room quickly faded.

That's the loop we're in now as agencies. If our future is tied to only making stuff, we're going to be on a perpetual roller coaster financially. That's always been a facet of agency life, but now the dips are going to come faster and run deeper until the next new thing emerges. Then we'll enjoy the temporary spike before the next stomach-flipping drop.

It also completely reduces our agencies to vendor status. We won't be invited to the C-suite table, and we won't get to compete based on our smarts. Instead, we'll be forced to compete on speed and price.

We've got to figure out a way to get paid for something more than making stuff. We were on that path before the recession, and now, the urgency is greater than ever. We don't want to be mere monkeys in the back of the room, banging out deliverables for pennies. Clients are demanding returns-on-investment (ROI) for their marketing spend, and without a strong strategy, we all know how that works out.

An even greater threat to our existence is the concept of cranking out content simply because the scope of work calls for five blog posts this month. Churning out generic content influenced Google 20 years ago. Today, there's simply too much out there. If we can't use content strategy to truly differentiate, then what we produce just becomes unproductive noise. And if it's yet another list post or some other fluff piece, the client can go to one of the many online writer factories and buy the same thing for a fraction of our cost.

This is the state of our world today, and this reality is as true for our agencies as it is for our clients. We, too, have to be findable, and once we're found, be easy to distinguish from the other agencies out there. Generic content isn't going to get us there.

We know that on the surface, it looks like we're painting a gloomy picture, so it might surprise you to hear that we're super psyched that this is the fork in the road. The opportunity for agencies is enormous— if we step into it.

We are entering the era of the authority. While you may already be sick of the phrase "thought leader," the truth is there aren't that many of them in our industry. Thought leaders don't write content that any other agency could claim. Thought leaders don't write about anything and everything, and thought leaders don't compete on price.

And their time is now.

For the last two decades, the global PR agency Edelman has conducted research that examines who and what consumers trust and how that trust influences their buying behaviors. They recently released the 2019 Trust Barometer, and the results are incredibly telling about whom consumers trust today and whom we see as a credible authority. This is a worldwide study with 33,000 consumers from 27 countries participating.

One of the biggest takeaways from this year's study is that consumers assign a high level of trust to people they believe are "just like me." When you think about the influence that ratings, reviews, and influencers have with their audiences, you begin to see the power of that belief.

But this research isn't about the celebrity influencer. This study is documenting the rise of the common man influencer. It's noteworthy because it gives statistical validity to the idea of "real people" as influencers and the impact they can have on behalf of a brand.

The research asked participants to rank what attributes made an influencer believable and trustworthy. The relatability of the influencer was nearly twice as important as the influencer's popularity. In other words, when consumers could see themselves in an influencer, they were far more likely to follow and trust that influencer. It's not about having millions of followers; it's about being someone you can relate to and connect with. For this very reason, if you're an agency, and you've been avoiding putting together a content strategy where you share your depth of expertise in your niche with the world, you need to re-think that decision.

Want to know what made an influencer even more compelling to the research participants than relatability? The one attribute that ranked higher than the trust we have in "people like me" is the trust we have in highly educated experts. The only three groups of people we trust more than people like ourselves are company, industry, and academic experts.

I want to make sure you saw that sentence: the only people we trust more than ourselves are experts. Experts are afforded the highest level of confidence and trust because they have a depth of knowledge in a specific industry or niche. So why in the world wouldn't we capitalize on that, as opposed to writing generic marketing tip posts that look like every other agency's content?

Agencies can't fake it anymore. We are at the end of the era when it was acceptable for agencies to promise effective content and produce something generic. If we can't do it for ourselves through a method we can monetize, and we can't do it in a way that uniquely defines us, we aren't going to be able to credibly sell our content for much longer.

Why would a client hire us to do what we can't do for ourselves? They'll either hire someone else or take the job in-house. We can't be generic, or we're going to get lost in the noise.

Beyond that, we're leaving money on the table. We can be influencers ourselves. We can earn the trust of our prospects so that we shorten the sales cycle and actually attract the best client candidates right to our door!

Here's the upside of where we are today. We're all in this together. Very few agencies have propelled themselves out of this perpetual loop, so there's time for you to choose a different path for your agency and your clients. You can be one of the early adopters if you're ready to boldly step out.

We're at the cusp of a huge shift, and if you take full advantage now, you're going to be tough to catch. You could be a Benton & Bowles-like trendsetter, which will put you back into the C-Suite and give you double-digit profitability. You can own an authority position that will future-proof your agency.

Are you ready to be part of this next generation of breakout agencies?

Chapter Two: Three Essentials to Becoming an Authority

(Drew)

If you were asked to think of an authority on any subject, who would come to mind? What about them designates them as an authority? What's true about them? And what does someone have to do to earn and keep the title of authority?

- They have a focus area or subject-matter expertise.

- They don't just repeat what everyone else is saying.

- They have a public presence where they share their expertise.

- They don't stray from their area of expertise—think specialist versus generalist.

- They aren't equally attractive to everyone. In fact, they probably bore most people to tears.

- They're significant—which is different from prolific—in terms of content creation.

- They don't create any generic content that someone with far less knowledge or experience could have just as easily written.

- They're perceived as an educator in some way.

- They have a passion for their subject matter.

- They have a strong point of view, which is the foundation of all of their content.

A true authority has something specific to teach us, and they want to be helpful or illuminating. They're eager to share what they know because they have a genuine passion for it, and they don't fear giving away the recipe to their secret sauce (or so it's perceived). That confidence and generosity is contagious. Their expertise is something specific groups of people (their sweet-spot prospects) are hungry to access. Call them an expert, a thought leader, an authority, a sought-after pundit, advisor, or specialist. They're all words for the same thing—a trusted resource who has earned that trust by demonstrating and generously sharing the depth of their specialized knowledge over and over again.

One way to recognize an authority is the ability to define them in a single sentence, like Simon Sinek. He's "the why guy." Brené Brown is "the dare-to-be-vulnerable woman." They've so narrowly and so carefully defined their expertise that we can capture it with a word or phrase. Does Simon Sinek talk about other things? Of course. But he always ties it back to his thing—the "why." Does Brené Brown write about additional topics? Absolutely. But she always deftly loops it back to being vulnerable and the power that comes from being brave enough to embrace vulnerability.

Beyond that, a true authority has a strong point of view or belief that influences how they talk about their subject area. A narrow niche, a strong point of view, and being findable in multiple places are the hallmarks of an authority position. Let's take a closer look at each element.

Narrow is Gold

The first essential in creating an authority position is recognizing that the narrower your audience, the better. It allows you to be quickly discovered and identified as someone your target audience needs to pay attention to, all because you're speaking their language. Ultimately, this means you can build an audience much faster. Once you've built the audience, and you genuinely know them and what they need, you can provide additional value by creating products and services you can sell.

If you choose to keep serving everyone as a generalist, you can still absolutely monetize a more generic position of authority (marketing expertise, for example), but if you want to get to this more quickly, you need to be ruthless in terms of focus.

It seems counter-intuitive. Our industry has focused on quantity in terms of audience for a very long time. Many people believe they need a massive audience to hit their sales and financial goals. As agency people, we know that's not true. We know that we're actually in a much better position if we're in front of the right micro audience where nearly everyone is aligned with the organization's ideal persona.

And yet, when it comes to our own business development efforts, we toss out a huge net, hoping that the right species of fish will swim in so we don't go hungry. Intellectually, we get it, yet our choices and behaviors often suggest we're still focusing on quantity, not quality.

You don't need a million downloads to get your podcast sponsored. You don't need to speak at 50 conferences to have someone walk up and ask you some questions that lead to a proposal. And you don't need to be on the bestseller list to use your book as an amazing business development tool.

Most agencies get this completely backward. They create broad, generic content as opposed to something that captures the interest of their ideal prospects. The content is fluffy and doesn't invite anyone to ask questions or lean in to learn more. But when an agency hones in on their specific audience and ignores the rest of the world (remember, one of the traits of an authority is that most people could care less about their content), the audience does lean in. They do ask questions, and they will eventually put you on a shortlist of agencies to consider.

And when you do it exceptionally well, you will be the *only* agency they consider.

Point of View

Here's what we know for sure. Our industry and the world around us are both experiencing change at an unfathomable rate, and it's only going to get faster. How we communicate nowadays, at best, is on the fly. But the one thing that will not change is that unique cocktail that defines our authority position. It's the combination of our area of expertise with the strong point of view we apply *to* that area of expertise. Our point of view is what we know to be true, and it's this truth that defines how we approach the work and how we add value.

For example, AMI's point of view is that most agency owners are accidental business owners. They were top-notch account service people, creatives, etc., but they haven't been exposed to the lessons they need to run their business profitably. AMI's depth of expertise is knowing the best practices, financial metrics, and sales techniques that allow agencies to thrive. When we layer that point of view, that most agency owners are accidental business owners, on top of our knowledge and expertise, it's easy to see how and where we can be of help. It tells us whom to serve and how to best serve them.

That's evergreen. And your agency should have a similar combination. Every agency needs to have an opinion about the work they do on behalf of their clients. We need a strong point of view about the marketplace, our audience, or our product or service.

As we fight for a prospect's attention, we must differentiate ourselves. We've got to plant a flag in the ground and claim ownership. We have to stand out against the sea of competitors. That authority position— our area of expertise plus our strong point of view—becomes the flag we plant. It is us laying claim to what is uniquely ours—the ability to serve a specific industry, niche, audience, etc., because of what we know and what we believe. It holds us firmly in place no matter what else changes. It becomes part of our differentiation equation. And we need both halves of the whole.

Without the point of view, even industry-specific content becomes claimable by others. Granted, it narrows the field, but there are certainly other agencies who work in the same industry or niches that you do. If we can take your agency's content (blog posts, white paper, podcast interviews, etc.) and swap another agency's logo for yours without anyone noticing, your content isn't as unique to you as you'd like. That's what we mean by claimable.

But don't get too overly focused on this. We aren't suggesting you're going to create an authority position no other agency on the planet can replicate. Odds are, no matter what your authority position, a handful of other agencies could claim it as well. But that's your goal—a small handful, rather than every agency out there.

Just to be clear, your point of view is the truth you overlay onto your niche or industry-specific expertise. It's an insight that influences the work you do. For example, in my agency, our unique point of view is that clients need to invert their typical spending model. Rather than spending the majority of their budget chasing prospects, we believe they should spend the lion's share of their budget on their existing customers.

We then take that point of view and marry it with our industry niches (companies that sell to insurance companies, banks, or credit unions) to differentiate ourselves, even among the other agencies who also have expertise in the same niches.

The ideal scenario for building your authority position is one in which you have the one-two punch of a point of view paired with that narrow audience or topic area. That's a powerful combination. You can carve out a more superficial authority position with just one of the two elements, either a point of view or niche expertise, but the consequence is, if you're going to only include half of the one-two punch, you're going to share your unique position with more agencies.

A strong point of view can absolutely be a specific belief about some aspect of your niche. It can absolutely be a belief about the clients or the industry you serve. For some agencies, their point of view is built around a depth of understanding for a specific audience like millennials or the LGBTQ community.

There will be some of you who just don't want to specialize. You want to be the generalist and mostly serve clients within a specific geographical area. If that's you, it's even more critical that you have a unique point of view. Otherwise, you risk being viewed as a completely generic choice. To avoid being painted by that brush, you've got to have a distinct point of view or methodology that will genuinely differentiate you from your local competitors.

You also want to make it clear that you're a generalist by choice. You're like a country doctor who takes care of people from birth to death. When you work across many industries you need to know a little bit about everything. Try building a point of view around that truth to support your generalist choice.

If you work with the local butcher, the baker, and the candlestick maker, you know that there's a candlestick maker specialist agency out there somewhere, pitching that they know the candlestick business better than anyone. Your point of view has to combat that "hire a specialist" argument.

At some level, you probably already know what your agency's point of view is, but you don't recognize it as such. Odds are, you either take it for granted because you talk about it so often, or you just need to dig a little deeper to find the gold in what you're already teaching, talking about, and using to build client recommendations.

When you walk yourself through the triggers in this chapter and define your point of view, you're probably not going to say, "I'm shocked! I would never have guessed that's what it was!"

You just have to peel the onion back several layers to get to something that's genuinely different enough that you can own it.

You Can't Be a One-Trick Pony

Essential number three is that an authentic authority is not a one-trick pony. That means you can't create content so narrow it only works on one channel. An expert doesn't have just one book. Or just a podcast.

You can't place all of your bets on one horse (or pony, to stick with our theme).

The problem is that whatever pony you rode in on is not going to be the popular pony forever, and you can't rely on all of your prospects consuming that specific channel. You need to be more findable, which means you need to have your authority-positioned content in more than one place. If you're going to build this position for your agency, you have to answer the question, "How does my point of view come to life across multiple channels?"

Your goal is to create the impression that you're everywhere. The good news is that it doesn't take that many channels to make that happen. You need a cornerstone channel and some cobblestones.

When we say cornerstone content, what we mean is content that's big and meaty, so it can be sliced and diced into smaller pieces of content—what we call cobblestones. The definition of cornerstone is the first stone placed. When you're constructing a building, you carefully set that first stone because you know all the other stones will be set in reference to the cornerstone. When you take that cornerstone content and break it up into infographics, quote cards, blog posts, tweets, guest appearances on someone else's podcast, etc., that's your cobblestone content. The combo of your niche expertise and your unique point of view should be woven into every piece of content you create. In some cases, it will be overt, and in other cases, subtle. But it should always be present to some degree.

A smart example of this style of content was developed by an AMI network member, Springboard Healthcare Marketing. Agency owner Rob Rosenberg and his team have built cornerstone content around doing primary research focused on the power of a strong brand for healthcare-related organizations. They conduct primary research and publish the results. The research data and the reports built from it are their cornerstone. From that cornerstone, they consistently create cobblestones of content on their website's blog, in speeches Rob gives at healthcare conferences, and during podcast appearances.

As you might imagine, they also share all of those content elements on their social media channels to create interest in both their cornerstone and cobblestones. People doing Google searches might land on a specific blog post (a cobblestone) which references the overarching research (the cornerstone) and links back to it. Each piece builds on the others, and all of them drive the agency's specific point of view, which is tied to what they call "heartbeat brands."

Some experts or influencers try to be everywhere, but that stretches them pretty thin pretty quickly. All you need are a few channels spot-on for your audience that you consistently feed with new content. Your agency will need a single cornerstone and at least two or three cobblestone channels. From there, you can use your social media channels to spotlight both.

Just remember, your cornerstone is the primary channel through which you consistently deliver useful content that helps your audience do their jobs better. And it needs to be meaty enough that you can slice and dice it into multiple cobblestones.

Think of the cobblestones as snack-sized pieces of content (a quote graphic featuring your podcast guest, for example) that someone might stumble upon and become interested enough that they are led to your cornerstone content. You need both. But you don't need dozens.

Cornerstones, by their nature, require a much more significant time investment, which means you don't have time to create too many. Far better to do one exceedingly well than to stretch yourself too thin, and better to be consistently present in a few places as opposed to occasionally showing up everywhere. You know this because you say it to your clients every day. But that doesn't mean you're immune to the trap.

You want to build something you can sustain for the long haul, and unless you're going to make being an authority your full-time gig, better to start with one.

Your cornerstone, and at least a few of your cobblestones, need to be built on media you own and control, not on someone else's platform. That might be your agency's website, a book you write, research you conduct, or your own podcast series.

You can use channels like Instagram, a Facebook page, Reddit, or Twitter to highlight your efforts, but your cornerstone content shouldn't be housed there. You don't want to go to the effort of creating content only to have some third party (like Facebook) decide to take it down or charge people for accessing it.

While you don't want to build your cornerstone content on a media channel that you don't own, that doesn't mean you don't want to be on other people's channels. If your cornerstone content is targeted and tied to your point of view (POV), and you're consistent in creating smaller pieces of content from that cornerstone, you're going to get noticed. That's all you need to get invited onto other people's channels.

One of the key elements about being an authority is that you don't want everything to remain on your owned channels. You want to leverage other people's spheres of influence, and when you appear as a guest on their show or whatever channel they own and control, now they're endorsing you, telling other people how smart you are, and introducing you to an entirely new audience.

That amplification expands your audience exponentially once you have built the foundation that earns the invites. But they will roll in, in a variety of ways.

You'll be invited to:

- speak at conferences
- be a guest on podcasts
- write bylined articles for publications
- sit on a panel of experts
- serve on a board
- write a regular column
- teach a class
- be part of a webinar series
- be interviewed as a source by the media

And that's just the tip of the iceberg.

On occasion, your cornerstone channel will shift. This shouldn't be because you're indecisive or getting bored. It should be driven by your audience, reactions to your efforts, and potentially, media consumption trends. The content itself doesn't shift, but how you deliver the content might.

When I started executing this strategy for AMI, my writing was the cornerstone channel. I was creating a lot of content for the blog and was being published in publications like Forbes, Entrepreneur, or AdAge about once a month. I'd write content on the AMI website pointing to those articles, so they lived both on other people's channels and AMI's. But when we launched the Build A Better Agency podcast in 2015, it quickly eclipsed the writing and took the cornerstone channel position.

Interesting, that the main cobblestones (conference presentations, our AMI newsletter, shorter pieces of written content, etc.) have remained the same.

In a later section of the book, we'll walk you through the decision-making process of defining your cornerstone channel. From there, you'll have a plan to protect yourself against becoming a one-trick pony.

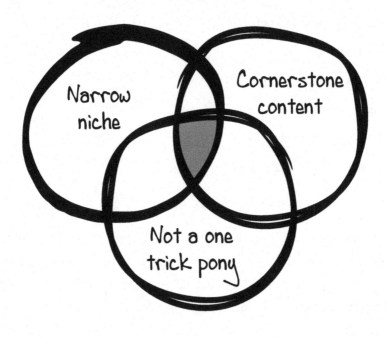

Chapter Three: Go Narrow to Monetize

(Stephen)

Our industry cut its teeth on the idea of casting a wide net, with the goal of exposing the message to as many people as possible. It was called mass media for a reason. But as technology made personalization possible, media channel options quadrupled, and we had data that allowed us to micro-target. Our language, strategy, and recommendations shifted as we helped clients build their marketing efforts.

We understand the idea of minimizing waste and only targeting the people who are potential customers when it comes to our clients. But when it comes to our own agencies and bank accounts, it's tough to ignore any dollar. Even a bad one. This idea that every dollar is a worthwhile pursuit is one of the misconceptions that often derails our business development efforts. By going a mile wide and an inch deep, we deplete our resources before we can have any impact.

Instead of going wide and attempting to attract a broad audience by writing generic content that is suitable for everyone, true authorities do the reverse. They confidently niche down and go narrow, which allows them to also go deep. There's nothing superficial about the substance of their content, its relevance, or its helpfulness because their cornerstone content is micro-targeted to that particular audience—it's gold!

As we said in Chapter Two, no true authority is a one-trick pony, and because of that, they teach from a depth of expertise, and there's always plenty to teach and share. They've studied and acquired their knowledge by being a practitioner in their industry. They've had real-world success as well as a few colossal failures. And they teach lessons from both. Thanks to their comprehensive body of work, they offer their audience content that can't be found anywhere else with the same quality, depth, frequency, or concentration.

That's you. You've been successfully doing this for a while. You've amassed success stories and compelling case studies. You've learned the industry (or audience or business problem) well and speak their language. And you know how to do it better than most. That's the basis for assuming an authority position.

In their book Niche Down, co-authors Christopher Lochhead and Heather Clancy wrote, "Become known of a niche you can own. That way, others will follow you. Others will be compared to you versus you being compared to others. That's a good thing. You'll be the person who changes people's thinking with a different point of view."

You all know that there are clients out there who just aren't the right fit for your agency. If you've been in business for more than a year, odds are good that you've already had at least one of them on your client roster and paid the price for ignoring your gut and agreeing to serve them.

When somebody slaps a big bag of money on the table and says, "We need you," it's hard to resist that temptation. We talk ourselves into making an exception, even though we have a bad feeling. This time, it will be different. We really need the money. We can change them or reset their expectations.

We ignore that nagging in the back of our head, and it costs us every single time. It may be awesome for a while. We may make great money, but in the end, we can't make them happy without paying a significant price. Those wrong-fit clients always end up costing us more than what we earn in terms of profitability, team satisfaction, and sometimes sleepless nights.

Keep in mind, you don't need a hundred new clients. If you target clients who are 10 percent or more of the annual adjusted gross income (AGI), two wins becomes a huge year for you. Even if all your wins don't end up being that significant in terms of AGI, three or four is a good growth year. Given that we don't play a volume game, why would we settle for less-than-ideal clients or agree to serve a client that ultimately, we know we can't satisfy?

We encourage you to niche down and go narrow with your cornerstone content for two critical reasons:

1. You will attract clients who are a perfect fit that you are set up to wow every day. Attracting those types of prospects will shorten your sales cycle and lengthen the number of years you happily serve those clients.

2. You will shorten the time it takes for you to monetize your content in a variety of ways, each one driving revenue back into your agency.

You can see how creating content around specific niches and making sure that your prospect list lines up within those niches can improve your ability to meet and exceed your business development goals. Be brave enough to stay narrow.

To be clear, we're not talking about that "lucky-strike extra" or those clients who walk into your door with a referral. We're talking about potential clients you're actively pursuing through your business development efforts and the right-fit prospects you're attracting with your cornerstone content. If you're going to take the time and effort to put out the bait, you want to be sure to catch the right animal, right? Focusing your cornerstone content so it serves your niches helps you do just that.

Unfortunately, most agencies haven't done this. They approach the broad market with very generic content, thinking it's thought leadership. In an attempt to get noticed, they create general marketing content based on the same trends article or Pantone color of the year announcement that every other agency is also producing.

That shallow, inch-deep content doesn't propel your agency where you want it to go. It doesn't move you forward because every other agency on the planet is writing that same type of pablum blog post, airing the same generic podcast episode, or whatever other content they hope passes for authority. But it does not pass the test for true thought leadership.

So let's address the second important reason to niche down when it comes to your cornerstone content. When you do, you shorten the time it takes to monetize your content.

If you want to monetize your efforts quickly, narrowing your focus to serve a niche audience is a crucial ingredient to success. Because when you serve a niche, you don't need a million downloads a month for your podcast. You don't need 500,000 subscribers to your YouTube channel. And you don't need 100,000 email subscribers.

That's a bit counterintuitive, but think value, not volume.

Whether you're going to monetize by winning more business or through tactics like selling sponsorships to your cornerstone content, you will be found more quickly and deemed more relevant if you go an inch wide and a mile deep. For example, another AMI agency, Brand Outcomes, does a lot of work in the trucking industry, and they have deep expertise in helping trucking companies recruit and retain drivers. They have taken their agency narrow to serve a specific audience and business problem.

They decided to launch a podcast as their cornerstone content hub. Within three months of airing their very first episode, they had already monetized their podcast by converting a guest into a substantial client. Their podcast enjoys about 400 downloads per month because the content is incredibly narrow. But every one of those 400 subscribers is exactly the right audience for their agency.

Later, a software company that wanted to reach decision-makers within the same trucking industry began to listen to the podcast and approached the agency to discuss sponsorship. Please notice: the agency did not initiate the conversation. The brand sought out the agency because of the depth of their expertise and the fact that their podcast came with very little audience waste if someone wanted to speak to the trucking industry.

At the time of this book's publication, they were still negotiating, but the sponsorship may well deliver six figures in annual revenue to the agency. None of this would have happened, or at least have happened so quickly, had the agency not been brave enough to launch a podcast that was unapologetically über-niched.

Don't miss the opportunity to leverage your cornerstone content. Think about creating content that will get you in front of your hottest prospects. If fact, the creation phase is an excellent time to connect with them. When cornerstone content is created correctly, it can act like what we call the "Trojan horse of sales" at my agency—Predictive ROI. We will cover the Trojan horse as a monetization strategy in Chapter Twelve, but here's a quick preview.

The idea is, you use your cornerstone content channel to create a relationship with your prospects by featuring them as your guests. The same people who will dodge or ignore your business development calls, emails, etc., will welcome your call when you're offering to put them in the spotlight and focus on their successes. This is one of the reasons why building an audience becomes critical. The more specialized your audience, the more attractive it will be for your prospects to get in front of them.

Whether you host a podcast, are writing a book, or are doing a video interview series, you can invite your prospects to be featured, which allows you to get to know one other in a non-sales environment.

You're creating a relationship with them, and next thing you know, they're asking you, "What is it you do again for your clients? Oh. Could you do that for me?" You don't have to sell at all. They sell themselves!

We see this strategy work time and time again for agencies that have built their content to serve this sales function, as well. They're not only selecting the right people to feature as part of their content, they've also structured the questions, so it actually becomes a biz-dev conversation. Naturally, they're doing it in a way that doesn't make their guests feel like they're being sold.

This is one of the ways this content strategy blends with your biz-dev strategy. Whether you're most comfortable writing articles, recording audio, or shooting video, identifying and interviewing your ideal prospects can make creating super-niched and valuable content easy because ultimately, it's not about your smarts, it's about theirs.

You're leveraging their smarts to create content for yourself, establishing a relationship with your ideal prospects, and when you publish the content, they love you for the exposure and for positioning them as an expert.

All of a sudden, you're no longer an agency owner looking for a new account. You're a journalist representing a media channel with an audience. Your prospect says yes to your invitation, as opposed to saying no to your biz-dev call.

Your cornerstone content acted as your Trojan horse. The company's gatekeeper opened the door and wheeled your agency right into the C-suite. And there you are, interviewing the decision-maker.

We're seeing this happen over and over and over again with agencies leveraging their cornerstone content. In three years, it's driven over $2 million in AGI into my agency, via our Onward Nation podcast.

The Trojan horse tends to be one of the fastest paths to monetization, but for it to work, you need a very finite and targeted prospect list so you can be intentional about whom you invite to participate. And that's difficult to do without a clearly defined POV and the boldness to go narrow.

Whether you deploy the Trojan horse of sales or not, don't be afraid to niche. That's where all the gold is.

Chapter Four: Defining Your Point of View

(Drew)

When I talk with agencies about niching, they immediately go to the industry or industries they should serve. And that is undoubtedly part of the equation. But it's not enough.

There are many agencies in your region of the world. Thousands of them, probably. You begin to narrow the competitive landscape when you identify how you will define your area of specialty. Will it be by industry, by audience, or by the business challenges you solve? That's your subject matter expertise. As we mentioned in the last chapter, that is the first hit in your one-two punch.

You, as well as everyone on your team, also need to give a rip. If you don't have a passion for the people you serve, you won't be able to consistently go above and beyond for them, no matter how deep your expertise. If another agency with the same expertise has a fire in their belly and thinks of the client's business as if it was their own, they'll eat your lunch every time.

I do not believe we can be successful if we put only our heads in the game. It's a heart-and-soul business, and it's why some of your clients have stuck with you for five, 10, 15, or more years. They not only want to know what you know, but that you care about their goals as much as they do. After all, their job or business is on the line. I don't blame them for wanting that.

But when you add the third element, a strong point of view, now you have shrunk the pool to almost no other agency but yours. When someone is hiring an expert, they want that expert to not only have core knowledge (cold, hard facts), but an opinion or interpretation of those facts. What do the facts mean? What truth is underlying the industry, audience, or problem-solving knowledge?

When you have all three of these elements, you've changed the game to be incredibly lopsided in your favor.

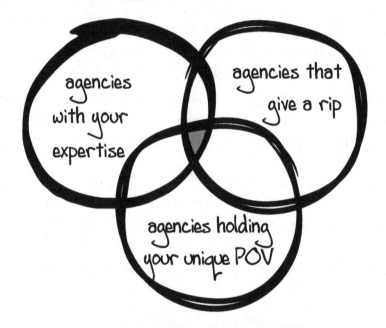

Your agency has a point of view, even if you can't articulate it yet. You may not think of it in clear terms or define it as such currently, but somewhere underneath the daily grind at the agency, you have some core beliefs that are woven through your recommendations and the guidance you provide to clients.

This point of view (as we mentioned in Chapter Two) is one of the critical elements of building your unique position in the marketplace.

If you can define which niches you want to focus on and have a heart for, that will put you ahead of more than 70 percent of all agencies. But when you wrap those niches into your point of view, now you are in the 5 percent category of differentiation. Very few agencies will be able to match your positioning if you truly own both the niches and the POV.

Every agency owner I know has a handful of phrases, stories, or anecdotes they use as they mentor young staff, pitch a prospect, or help a client understand why the agency has made a particular recommendation. This is one of those "it sounds easy, but it's tough" challenges. It helps to collect what I call your agency's "legendary stories"—those stories of glory you love to tell when you want to illustrate a point, demonstrate your value, or celebrate a victory on behalf of a client. Underneath those phrases, stories, and anecdotes are some core beliefs about marketing, connecting with an audience, and what it means to have success in business. Think of it as a foundational belief that supports your approach to the work you do for clients.

Now, how do you uncover it and articulate it? If you do any branding work for clients, you know their brand is buried deep within the organization, and it's your job to peel back the layers until you get to the gooey center. That's the same methodology you should employ here. Take inventory of those stories, anecdotes, legends, and key phrases you find yourself telling time and time again. Look for common threads and truths.

To look for some clues, ask yourself these questions:

- What truths have you learned that influenced your work?
- What recommendations do you always make?
- What stories do you always tell?
- What examples do you consistently use with clients, or how do you

uniquely serve your clients?

- What do you do that most agencies or businesses would never do?

Another way to discover your POV is to play what I call "the toddler why game." It usually takes two to four levels of why to get to that kernel of truth.

Look at a consistent reality that comes loaded with some significant challenges your core audience or niche wrestles with regularly. For example, my clients (agency owners) don't like to sell, and to avoid selling, they rely on referrals and organic growth, which comes with some inherent disadvantages and risks. Then, list the less-than-desirable outcomes of this truth. Sticking with our example, it might be:

- They experience high highs and low lows when it comes to an influx of new revenue from new clients.
- They are forced to serve or accept whichever prospects walk in the door through referrals as opposed to being able to design their business or attract only sweet-spot clients.
- They have no control over when new opportunities present themselves.
- Because their customers can and do come from everywhere, it's challenging to define a niche or area of expertise.
- I'm sure I'm just scratching the surface, but you get the idea.

Then start the toddler why game, which might play out like this:

Q: Why is the client willing to accept all of these consequences that make running their business more difficult?

A: Because either they don't know how to sell, don't like to sell, or don't believe in their ability to sell.

Q: Why?

A: Because they dislike rejection, and it's challenging to earn someone's attention. It's impossible to know when a prospect is getting ready to make an initial purchase, so they don't know who to target. No one wears an "I'm about to hire someone like you" sign on their forehead, and it's easy to avoid doing something you don't like by focusing on the daily fires inside the business.

Q: Why?

A: The buying cycle is unpredictable because in many cases the dollar amounts are large, the level of trust required to initiate the partnership is enormous, and the risks to the buyer (getting fired if the partner doesn't perform) are daunting. Therefore, the buyers tend to be skittish. They are also higher-level executives who aren't likely to take random sales calls from people they don't know.

Q: Why?

A: The risks are huge, which is why buyers tend to reach out to the vendor or partners they've always worked with or at the very least, already know or have had a referral connection to. They aren't likely to put their jobs on the line without some reassurance that the partner actually knows their stuff.

After several rounds of why, you will get to some facts or insights that will require some diagnosis on your part. If all of these things are true, what does it suggest or tell you? What can you conclude, learn, or change to break this pattern? Where is the faulty logic or assumption that puts you and your clients into this spot?

To wrap up this example, you might have concluded that given the realities of the buyer and the disadvantages of referral-only selling, there has to be a better or different way. What if your clients were recognized by the industry in which they work as subject matter experts? Add to that, what if others were also singing their praises and passing along their content that put a spotlight on their expertise?

Could this result in them enjoying the benefits of being pre-qualified as a trusted resource and generating so many inquiries that they could pick and choose which inbound leads to pursue based on their definition of a sweet-spot client? The answer, of course, is yes.

On top of that, because they are a subject matter expert, they could develop a cornerstone channel and an audience that would also be attractive to their best-fit prospects and use that to create connections with potential buyers on a whole different scale and level.

My POV from this exercise could be (and is) that the best way to sell today is to be seen as an authority in your field, and to use that platform of expertise to connect with buyers by inviting them to be a part of your trusted inner circle in channels you own and control. From that vantage point, you can demonstrate that you have a genuine passion for their world, and your unique point of view will help them accelerate past their competitors.

If you're not sure where to even start with the toddler why game, ask yourself these kinds of questions:

- We're able to help our clients because we know what truths about their industry?

- What do our clients' customers have in common?

- What mistake do we see prospects making that we immediately seek to course-correct for them?

- What is a shared experience or belief that our clients (or our clients' customers) have that we think is missing the mark?

- Do the people we serve have a common background, experience, or belief that gets in the way of their success?

- If we could wave a magic wand and everyone we work with could share a universal understanding about something, what would we want it to be?

- What habit, pattern, or belief is commonly accepted that you know is actually getting in the way of your clients achieving their goals?

Once you have some thought-provoking answers, begin to explore them with a few rounds of asking why. Some will lead you nowhere. But at least one of them will lead you to an absolute that you can confidently stand on. From there, you mold how you want to articulate your point of view.

Let's look at some examples:

Agency One's POV: We believe that Mom is the decision-maker for all healthcare decisions, so she must be the primary audience for all marketing, whether she is the patient or not.

Agency Two's POV: Eighty percent of your net new revenue should come from existing customers, so you should spend 75 to 80 percent of your marketing budget on growing their business rather than chasing new customers.

Agency Three's POV: In today's 24/7 connected world, our clients have to be communicating with their customers in the now, so we embed an agency employee on-site so we can help clients react more quickly and plan more effectively.

Examples two and three are still a little generic. But if you marry either point of view with a specific niche or industry, the POV will naturally be narrowed to be more definitive and unique to your agency.

For example, Agency Three's POV could become, "In today's 24/7 connected world, and because of the immediate nature of air travel issues, our airline clients have to be communicating with their customers in the now. We believe to serve them best, we must embed an agency employee on-site so we can help them react more quickly and plan more effectively."

You can see how that combination could make an agency unique when compared to their competitors.

This combination of your POV and narrowly defined areas of expertise is the nucleus of your authority position. It's the foundation upon which you build your content strategy with the clearly defined goal of attracting the prospects you most want to serve.

If you've nailed down your niches and those two to three niches have some tangential relationship to one another, ideally you would apply that same point of view for all of your work and the clients you serve.

If your niches are borne more from your agency's history, existing clients, or some other factor that results in them all being strong enough to lean on, but they don't really relate to one another, that may mean you need to develop a separate point of view for each niche. All the more reason to try to find some connective tissue between those niches!

Here's where the bravery comes in. You have to be brave enough to plant your flag. This is where many agencies get stuck. You may have a strong opinion about the work you do. You may have a depth of expertise in a particular industry, with a specific audience or example after example of how you've solved the same challenge for many clients. But you don't boldly declare it because it means you're acknowledging that many potential clients aren't the ideal fit for your agency.

Don't let that fear of not being the agency for everyone keep you from planting your flag and owning that position. This authority positioning strategy is about attracting the right fit clients and proving to them, before you ever do a bit of work, that you're the agency that truly aligns with their industry, their goals, and their needs.

Once you have defined your POV and your niches, you now have the boundaries for your content. You're only going to create content that, in some way, connects to and reflects that positioning.

Now your content, regardless of the channel you choose, has a theme or story. Each piece builds on the others, and they all lead your audience to recognizing you as the XYZ agency. That positions you to be pursued by prospects rather than you having to chase after them.

If this all feels daunting, like you can't possibly discover your unique point of view, remember, this is not you inventing something new. This is recognizing a truth that you have operated under for a while. You just didn't label it as anything more than something you've always known or suspected. It may be a phrase you say just about every day or in just about every new business pitch, or it might be more subtle. But you've been operating with this knowledge for a while, conscious or not.

It's time to peel back the onion and claim it as a critical element of how you position the agency.

Chapter Five: Be More Than a One-Trick Pony

(Stephen)

Back in the late 1800s and early 1900s, the traveling circuses of the day were referred to as "dog and pony shows." The shows were given that name because they featured trained dogs and ponies as main attractions. These dog and pony shows were also credited with the origin the colloquial phrase still commonly used today, "one-trick pony," because of what happened to The Cuffling Circus when they were performing in Oregon in 1905.

One of the Cuffling performances did not go well. The featured act that evening involved a pony that, unfortunately for both the circus and the audience, knew just a single trick. He could play dead. It was cute the first time, but as you might imagine, it was less impressive when repeated over and over. The audience demanded a refund, and the phrase "one-trick pony" was born.

So when we say that someone who owns an authority position can't be a one-trick pony, we mean they can't simply depend on a single go-to move or channel and call it a day. A true authority does the opposite. They've invested years perfecting their craft, have developed a depth of expertise, and have shared their knowledge generously in many places. They're typically fired up about sharing what they know and have a teacher's mentality about the importance of not holding their expertise so close to the chest. Also like a great teacher, they use a variety of teaching tactics, knowing that every student learns in different ways.

Someone who is a genuine authority doesn't rely on only one channel (their one pony) to build an audience because like a memorable teacher, they understand their audience needs a variety of ways to learn. They're focused on being helpful to their audience across multiple channels because this gives them the opportunity to impact more people, to create repetition (which aids learning), and to reduce the risk of losing the audience if and when a channel loses favor or relevance.

In today's hyper-competitive market for awareness and attention, you and your agency cannot afford to rely on just one channel, even if you're the host of a top-ranked podcast or author of a single best-selling book. When we talk about planting your flag into firm ground, what we're saying is that it shouldn't matter where your content appears; it should hold its own, today and into the future. Your authority position has to be channel-agnostic to survive the test of time.

Channels come and go pretty quickly these days, but a position of authority (the depth of expertise combined with a well-articulated point of view) weathers those changes. That authority position becomes a flag you can plant into any terrain, be it social media, speaking at conferences, writing a book, launching a podcast, or whatever the cool kids might be using in 2057.

Add to this the reality that we are multitasking media consumers today. We flit from a book to watching a ball game on TV to surfing the web to checking Instagram within a few minutes if we're layering those media outlets on top of each other at the same time. So as we said earlier, you want to create the appearance of being everywhere, not just in one place.

Just as small strands of thread are woven together to create a powerful rope, so too are all the channels that make up a strong hub-and-spoke strategy (another way of thinking of the cornerstone and cobblestones). You want to build your content strategy with multiple threads so that when one thread is weakened or breaks altogether, the whole structure isn't affected, and your mission can carry on. No matter how channels shift going forward, your thought leadership will drive the growth of your agency if you don't rely on a single channel.

The cornerstone and cobblestone model will make sure you're easily findable in the primary channels, no matter where your audiences go to get their information. I was recently a guest on a podcast, and during the pre-interview chat, the host was lamenting to me about how LinkedIn's Pulse Network (the social network's failed attempt at creating a business-to-business blogging platform) had gone defunct along with all the views, likes, comments, and website traffic the host had enjoyed before its demise. All of his efforts were lost because he made two cardinal mistakes. The first was choosing a channel he didn't own or control for his cornerstone. The second was he only focused on that one channel. When it collapsed, it wiped away everything he'd built.

Your content needs to be discoverable across multiple channels and ideally shared in numerous formats—long form, short form, written, audio, video, or whatever plays to your strengths, your audience's media consumption habits, and the creative abilities of your agency. Before you freak out, remember, this doesn't mean you need to create original content for each and every channel. You're going to be re-purposing and re-packaging key pieces to create that effect.

You're going to identify the core format or channel for your cornerstone content. That's the hub. Then you and your team are going to build spokes (cobblestones) off of the hub to protect yourself from being the one-trick pony.

The benefit of this strategy is that it gives your audience the impression that you're everywhere and that you've created content for every media channel. Really, you can create a single piece of cornerstone content (maybe you wrote a book or conducted some primary research) and then slice and dice it so you can share snippets of value in many different ways and places. And when a prospect meets you for the first time, your goal is to make them say, "Thank you. Every time I turn around, I see something helpful from you. Now that we've had a chance to interact, you're just what I expected you to be."

Remember, when we think about someone like Seth Godin, part of what makes him an expert in our eyes is our perception that his content can be found everywhere. But really, it's his cornerstone strategy with a few consistently fed cobblestones that creates that impression. Seth writes a new blog post every day and a new book every few years. Those are his cornerstone channels. But from there, his people create graphics with his quotes, he gets invited to be on podcasts, offers courses, and speaks at events.

We are not saying you need to be the next Seth Godin for this strategy to serve your agency well. And it doesn't have to be overwhelming. You aren't going to be producing cornerstone content every day, and you don't have to do this alone.

We're showing you how to get started. Then, over time, you'll add a few more channels as you gain traction with your POV and collect feedback from your audience, and after you and your team become more comfortable taking on more content-creation responsibilities. But it should never be about more for the sake of more. It should just be about discovering new ways you can make yourself helpful to your audience.

As we mentioned in Chapter Two, once you establish your expertise using a POV that is interesting and uniquely your own, you will get invited into other people's spheres of influence. Then they're the ones telling other people how smart you are and touting your expertise.

In 2009, Nicole Mahoney founded her agency Break the Ice (BTI) Media in Pittsford, New York. Nicole and her BTI team focus on helping destination marketers win by attracting more people to their communities. Nicole worked hard to build BTI's reputation, she and her team won several key accounts, and the agency grew over time. Like most agencies, they tried to juggle their content marketing like social media, blogging, occasionally writing an article, etc., but while they worked to keep these balls in the air, no single content stream acted as a genuine hub of cornerstone content upon which the agency could build a solid foundation.

Then, in 2016, Nicole made a game-changing decision. She decided to launch a podcast and make it the content hub for the agency. As the podcast grew in popularity, and Nicole stayed hyper-focused on her niche and POV combination, she earned the attention of her target industry's leaders. She got invited to take the show on the road at some of the biggest tradeshows in the travel and tourism industry. This gave her the opportunity to interview industry thought leaders (and BTI's most coveted prospects) while on-site at conferences and events. Each of the interviews were aired as special podcast episodes, and because she was on-site at the event, she could communicate with prospective guests pre-show, and then distribute the episode featuring those guests. Those connections all became strategic spokes centered around the hub of their podcast.

The value of the road show was that BTI's cornerstone was not only exposed to their own audience, but to the trade show and conference's audiences as well. Their core audience grew exponentially as cross-pollination began to happen. This is when you start to see a different trajectory for the distribution of your thought leadership content.

After recording each episode, BTI had 60 minutes of content that could be pared into smaller pieces and distributed to populate their cobblestone channels. Each podcast was broken into five to 10 additional elements. Do the math. If BTI produces 52 episodes (not counting their special on-site episodes) and an average of seven additional pieces from each podcast, that's more than 400 content elements that all prove that Nicole and her team eat, drink, sleep, and think about travel and tourism marketing every day of the year.

The ROI of this effort has been significant. Nicole and the BTI team have been invited several times into prospects' offices and awarded business without ever having to present or pitch for it. This was due simply to the strength of Nicole's POV and the reputation of her agency, which was demonstrated time and time again through their cornerstone content and its corresponding cobblestones.

That is the power of being a true authority, and you can do this for your agency, too.

Chapter Six: Creating Cornerstone Content

(Drew)

This is where many agencies and their clients miss the mark when it comes to content strategy. We get overwhelmed at the concept of having to create content on a consistent basis, so we err toward deciding to make a lot of little pieces of content as opposed to starting with something substantial. For some reason, 50 blog posts seem less daunting than one research project or writing a book.

You are going to read the word cornerstone so many times in this book, you're going to want to stab your eye with a pencil. You may already be at that point. But there's good reason for the repetition. Creating cornerstone content is the key to having the capacity to step into your rightful position of authority.

Let's dig into our definition.

Cornerstone content is:

- meaty enough to produce lots of smaller pieces of content.

- significant enough to serve as the epicenter of your promotion, activity, and eventual fame—in your circle of influence, of course; we aren't suggesting you'll become the next Beyoncé!

- consistent in how often you create content and how much you stay focused on one topic or area of subject matter.

- sales-free. This is about you teaching and helping. Stop. Period. End of story.

- all about building the audience. That's your primary goal.

- a long-term play. No one's going to recognize you as an authority after three months.

Now, let's unpack each of those.

Cornerstone content is meaty, dense content that gives us plenty of opportunities to slice and dice it into cobblestones. It needs to have significance. Depending on the channel you choose for your cornerstone content, you might only need to create it once a year or, in the case of a video or podcast series, upwards of once a week. This is dense content with lots of nuggets that can all stand on their own or foster further conversation. Take a research report, for example.

Let's say you decide your cornerstone content is going to be an annual study you do with a research partner because you want the results to have statistical validity. That research is always going to study something über-relevant to your audience, take into account your point of view, and be repeatable. It could be repeatable in that you do the exact same study year over year to compare the results. Or it could be repeatable in that you explore a new angle or topic for the same audience every year.

In your research, every question you ask, or each response to those questions, could turn into a blog post, a quote card, a factoid, an infographic, etc. Your research is dense with insights, information, and lessons to be learned. And with each piece of content you create, you demonstrate over and over again how uniquely in-tune you are with that specific audience.

But you can't do the same thing with a blog post or even a blog post series. There just isn't enough meat on the bone. Everything becomes one-and-done, and it's much more difficult to build a body of work you can stand on to claim your position of authority. But write a book, have an industry-specific podcast, or be the co-presenter of primary research with all of it laser-focused on the same thing, and now you're an authority.

The next characteristic of cornerstone content is that it can be the epicenter of your efforts. In other words, it can serve as a cornerstone in your cornerstone-and-cobblestone model and is big enough that you can promote it as such. Whether you're on a Facebook page or speaking at a conference, you want to be able to point back to your epicenter.

Think of your cornerstone content as the matriarch or patriarch of the entire village. Your cobblestones are the villagers of multiple generations, but they were all born from the original mother or father. As we'll explore later in the book, some of these cobblestones or supportive channels will be for marketing purposes, while others will be for monetizing your authority position. Think Instagram stream versus online courses.

As such, your cornerstone needs to live on a digital platform that you own if you are going to be consistently referring back to it. A Facebook group or series of scintillating articles on Medium are not safe options. You want to own and control your cornerstone and not be subject to the business decisions or whims of a third party. This shouldn't be something Mark Zuckerberg can derail after you've spent a couple of years building it out.

That doesn't necessarily mean you can't host the content with a third party (think YouTube or a podcast-hosting platform), as long as you own the content outright and no one can delete it or deem it out of the confines of a service agreement.

Consistency is often the tough one for agencies who start down this path. Just as it's the tough one for our clients when we try to help them embrace content creation. Everyone is enthusiastic in the beginning. It's a new toy, and everyone wants to play with it until it isn't new anymore. Then it's just another thing on the to-do list.

Top that off with the human truth that you'll get bored with the topic long before your audience does. I was at a James Taylor concert (the original JT, despite what agency owner Lori Highby of Keystone Click says!), and he was setting up for the song, "You've Got a Friend." He said, "I had no idea I would be singing this song every single night of my life for over 50 years!" I'm sure he's over it. But he also knows it matters to his audience and that it's part of his set of signature songs.

In 1948, pediatrician Dr. Benjamin Spock wrote *The Common Sense Book of Baby and Child Care*, which became an instant bestseller and by 1998 had sold over 50 million copies, making it the second-best-selling book of all time, with only the Bible beating it out for the number one spot.

Dr. Spock went on to write ten more books throughout his career. He also appeared on every talk show of the day when his first few books came out. Do you know what he talked about every single time? Some aspect of caring for babies and children.

Bottom line, this strategy will not work if you're not consistently producing something of value about your defined subject matter. If consistency is challenging, then resisting the urge to sell is almost torturous for most agencies. We can't seem to help ourselves. As though we're in a hypnotic trance and have no control, we have to stick in that last-minute appeal or offer. But we must resist this urge. Make no mistake about it, creating an authority position is part of the sales process. But in this phase of the sales process, we are solely creating and nurturing trust by being helpful.

I don't know about you, but nothing makes me flee from a store faster than an aggressive salesperson who keeps pestering me. That's what our sales pitches feel like at this stage. Sticking with my salesperson analogy, we need to organize our store so that buyers can come in and out at will and find what they need. They can easily initiate a conversation and ask us questions, but we don't hover or keep asking if they want to try something on. We've laid out our best stuff for them to peruse, and we're ready to be helpful if and when we're asked.

Just like what happens in a store, if someone is interested in buying something or asking more about what you do, they'll approach you. That subtle shift in roles is critical to your authority strategy's success. They're in the driver's seat now, which feels much more comfortable for them. If you want them to stick around to soak in your smarts, do not sell.

What you can and should do is lay those cobblestones very close together, so your audience naturally follows them deeper and deeper into your content. But nowhere along the path should there be a pushy salesperson.

The reason is simple. You want them to feel comfortable so they keep coming back. Your number one priority is to build your audience. Your ultimate goal is to create a community that knows, likes, and trusts you and gets such incredible value from you that they will ask to give you money just to get more value. The two questions that you must ask yourself every step of the way are:

1. How is this (strategy, piece of content, etc.) helping my audience get better at their job?

2. How is this (strategy, piece of content, etc.) building or deepening the connection to my audience?

If that strategy or specific piece of content doesn't generate a good answer for both questions, don't do it. Either re-tool it or shelve it.

Your audience is a precious and skittish lot. They expect you to try to sell them something right off the bat. They expect to be underwhelmed. They expect you to sell their name and email address. They expect you to be a one-trick pony or only trickle out good content every once in a while. Your task is to rise above every one of those expectations, every time. It sounds easy, given the low bar, but it's not. With your crazy calendar, the ups and downs of agency life, your hunger to sell, and about a million other reasons, this is hard stuff. We don't want to blow any smoke up your skirt about that. If this was easy, it wouldn't be so effective because everyone would do it. It requires discipline in every sense of the word.

But when you act as the guardian of your own audience, and you genuinely care about them and their success, the relationship is nothing short of amazing. They will think of you as someone they can count on to keep them on the right path. They will talk about you in a way that draws more people to you. They will support you financially by buying from you with confidence because you've proven to them that they can trust you.

The bigger the audience (within that narrow niche), the better. Your audience is the gateway to all the gooey goodness that comes from being an authority. Bigger fees, bigger stages, bigger connections, and bigger opportunities. But that audience can also pull the rug out from under you if they stop believing. Which means you need to be authentic. You need to come at this from a genuine desire to help, share, and teach. You need to re-earn their trust at every turn.

One of the most amazing compliments I receive is when someone attends one of our live workshops or sticks around to say hello after a conference speech, and they tell me, "I've been consuming your content for years, and I just wanted to meet you. You are exactly who I thought you'd be. Thank you for all you do to help agency owners like me. I have learned a ton." That's the level of trust and gratitude you can earn by being a true authority. That's the power of nurturing your audience and caring about their success. But, as you might imagine, that isn't earned overnight or with one blog post. You are in this for the long haul!

People always ask, "How long does it take?" The answer is yes. We can't give you a precise time frame, and for each of you, it's going to be different. There are so many factors, including:

- the consistency of your content creation.
- the quality of your content—are you saying something fresh or just repeating old news?
- the amount of time and effort you spend promoting your content.

- the hunger of your audience. Some are starving and will gobble up everything you share; others may be more satiated and will only consume the tastiest of offers.

- the level of competition. If you're writing about general healthcare marketing, for example, it's going to be a long haul; if you're writing about marketing to women over 50 with breast cancer, you'll have a much quicker adoption.

- lucky-strike moments like having someone else with a similar audience share your content in their world.

But, suffice it to say, this is not a get-rich-quick scheme. At a minimum, you should count on it taking six months to a year before you reap any significant benefit from your efforts. By year two, you should be dancing a jig at how well it's working, and by year three, you should be well-established as the authority you are.

On occasion, a single podcast episode or video or book will catapult someone into the spotlight and earn them a huge payout. But that's the exception, not the rule. Don't count on being the exception, or else you risk being so disappointed, you let it derail the effort.

The one element of defining cornerstone content we haven't covered yet is, what exactly are you going to be creating? What will be your opus?

We have some more exploration to do before you need to decide which specific type of cornerstone content is right for you and the agency, but here are the most common options:

- a podcast series (talking)
- authoring a book (writing)
- a primary research study (hybrid)
- co-authoring or crowdsourcing a book (writing)

- a video series featuring yourself or interviews with others (talking)
- a webinar series featuring yourself or a series of co-hosts (talking)
- provocative and prolific articles or blog posts (writing)
- keynote speeches that elegantly define your niche and POV, so you avoid the easy fall into the generalist trap (talking)

As you can see by looking at the list, creating any one of these leans heavily on either talking or writing. Most people gravitate to one or the other. On the writing side of the equation, you can be more deliberate and thoughtful. On the speaking side, no matter how well-prepared you are, there will be an element of improvisation that comes with the delivery. We'll dig into the pros and cons of both in the upcoming chapters so you can make an informed decision. But most people select one channel that feels the most like them or the most comfortable.

You need to think beyond what feels natural, but consider also what you will enjoy for the long haul. Remember, one of the tenets of success here is consistency. Even a book or research project isn't a one-and-done effort. If you're going to author books, you'll want to produce a new one every two or three years at the longest. Most research projects are annual studies. For you to establish yourself and your agency as an authority, consistency is a critical component. You're going to be doing this for a while, so choose wisely.

Of course, it isn't all about you. It seems pretty logical that you'll need to consider your audience when it comes to selecting which cornerstone deliverable makes the most sense. If your audience has made it very clear they aren't podcast people, then don't pick podcasting, even if you have always fancied yourself to be the marketing world's Casey Kasem. (If you're under 35, he was the original Shaggy from the Scooby Doo cartoons and about a million other recognizable characters.)

A third consideration is budget. Many of these options are absolutely doable from within your agency, with little to no outside expense. But some of them are tougher to DIY. Don't think only in terms of dollars, either. Think about all of your agency's resources—time, talent, and money—and decide how much you can budget for this project.

Some of you may be ambitious enough that when you look at the options, more than one channel looks appealing. Fight that urge. It's easy for your eyes to be bigger than your proverbial stomach here. We want you to be able to maintain this effort for a long time. One of the most common ways to trip up is to commit to more than you can comfortably produce for the long-run.

If you're familiar with my content for AMI, you may be thinking I'm a hypocrite right now. We violate the advice I just proffered and produce several of these. In our defense, we didn't start out committing to multiple cornerstone channels. We committed to one and didn't dive into the next until the first was so systematized, it made the second cornerstone much easier. Over time, one channel led to the creation of a second and third, and it seemed almost natural to expand the family, as it were. And some of our cornerstones (books, research) required heavy lifting only once a year, and sometimes less often, as is the case with books. In both of these examples, I was sharing the work with a strategic partner or co-author.

That's one of the other perks of an authority strategy. Other smart people will want to partner with you to create additional content. You get more bang for your buck, and only have to do half the work! I love that equation.

But our recommendation is still to adopt a slow and steady approach to this. One baby at a time, as opposed to trying for triplets.

Chapter Seven: The Pros and Cons of Talking

(Drew)

As we said in the previous chapter, you'll need to decide how you'd like to create your cornerstone content. You can either write (book, blog, articles, etc.), or you can speak (podcast, video, keynotes, webinars, etc.). It's important to note that for many of your options, you'll be doing a bit of both, but one side is usually dominant.

Very few people hop up on a stage and freestyle their keynote presentation. Many podcasters will write out their solocasts, or at the very least, outline them, before they hit the record button. But at some point, no matter how detailed your notes, you have to take the leap and start talking. The minute that happens, you are, to a certain extent, flying without a net.

There's an element of improvisation in creating a podcast (as with any long-form audio format), recording videos, speaking at events, or hosting webinars. It's not a singular activity. You have a guest or an audience or both. And they're going to throw a monkey wrench or two into your carefully planned content. That's a given.

For some of you, this might be a pro. You love the spontaneity and challenge of that unanticipated question or comment. For others, it's a big con. The unpredictability is terrifying. How you react to that factor may influence your decision.

Now is probably a good time to note that many people choose a primary platform (like hosting a podcast) with the intention of using that content to also create another cornerstone channel, like a book. Stephen's book, *Profitable Podcasting*, is an excellent example of this strategy. He outlined his book, then recorded solocasts and interviews to correspond with each chapter. Then, he transcribed the audio content, added in some additional examples and graphics, and voila, 90 percent of the book was done. But once the book was done, he kept on podcasting. It's still his primary channel.

Keep that in mind as you sort through the pros and cons of both writing and talking. One can undoubtedly lead to the other, but that's a temporary blip, and sooner or later you will go back to the primary channel. So it needs to be something you really want to keep doing for years. (And yes, I mean years. Remember, this is a long-term play.)

Choosing the writing side of the equation feels like the classic decision. Books and trade publications have been around forever, and being an author feels significant (because it is). Even blogging has been around for more than a decade.

The talking side of things feels more recent. Sure, we've had talk radio forever, but it's really the advances in Internet connectivity and communications technology that have made it possible for anyone to create on-demand, long-form audio podcasts, video series, and webinars. Standing on a stage has certainly been around for a while, but new venues like TED Talks have certainly made public speaking look shiny and new again.

Primary research is the one item on our list of potential cornerstone content channels that is a true hybrid of both. Odds are, you're going to be partnering with a research team or individual to create the tool, but you'll write many pieces based on research findings, and hopefully, you'll use the research to book yourself on podcasts, news interviews, and speaking gigs.

Let's look at the overarching pros and cons of the channels that rely primarily on speaking (podcasts/audio shows, video series, webinar series, and conference speeches), then we'll examine each option a little more closely.

PROs

- Element of improv.
- Faster to market (less prep).
- Your guests can help you create the content.
- If you have guests, you get to promote on their channels, too.
- Podcasting is hot and emerging as a hugely popular channel (you can still be an early adopter).
- Podcasting fits in with our multitasking nature.
- Inexpensive gear and setup (less than $5,000 for any speaking channel).

- In the case of audio and video, the audience can consume your product whenever they want, and binge-consume.
- You get to control the length of the content.
- You get to control the frequency of its release.

CONs

- Element of improv.
- Can spend too much time on vanity stages.
- You need some level of production quality.
- Video, when done badly, can hurt you.
- Speaking requires an invitation and travel.
- Requires some technical expertise and time commitment.
- Not a one-and-done channel. You have to keep producing to create a body of work.
- Can't be done at odd hours because it's rarely a solo effort (or you have a live audience).
- With speaking, you have to market yourself.
- Speaking requires a speaker one sheet, speaker reel video, etc.
- Much more difficult to encourage and facilitate subscriptions to videos (as you might with iTunes for podcasts).

The Realities of Podcasts and Audio Shows

Podcasting is hot right now, and there's no sign that the growth is going to slow down any time soon.

According to the 2019 Infinite Dial Study, research conducted by Edison Research and Triton Digital, considered to be the most significant research in the arena of digital media consumer behavior in the U.S., 197 million Americans are listening to online audio in 2019, which is 70 percent of the population. For the first time, according to the study, more than 50 percent of the U.S. population has listened to at least one podcast, and there are 17 million more monthly podcast listeners this year than there were in 2018.

Among the respondents who identified as podcast listeners (that is, they have listened to at least one podcast in the last seven days), they listen to an average of seven podcasts per week—per week! "Online audio has reached a new high in weekly time spent listening, potentially driven by podcasting and smart speakers," the research report declares. This is big news for us.

There are a few reasons for this growing popularity. The first is pretty obvious. Today, every consumer with a smartphone has all the technology and tools they need to be a podcast listener. Access today is simple, free, and always within our reach.

Another reason podcasts are so popular is because of the listener's ability to multitask when consuming the content. I hear from listeners who say I'm on the treadmill with them, walking their dog with them, on the commuter train with them, or that I'm part of their nine-hole golf routine. Given that time is such a scarce resource, this feature of podcasting is very appealing to people.

It also speaks to the need for good-quality audio that can be heard and understood over whatever else is going on, as well as the clarity of your message. I'm pretty sure that I rarely have 100 percent of my audience's attention, so I need to work hard to make sure they get the information they need in as clear and as memorable a way as possible.

In addition, the flurry of fiction, narrative, and entertainment-focused podcasts is good for us B2B podcasters as well. Podcasts like *Serial,* *This American Life,* and many of the true-crime podcasts introduce the masses to the medium. Once they get used to weaving podcasts into their routine, they start looking for podcasts that focus on a topic that matters to them.

One of the most compelling arguments for producing a podcast is the ability to micro-target an audience. In fact, it may be the best example of the power of well-niched marketing. Know who you can help 110 percent, and focus on them and only them. With the search functionality of any podcast app, consumers can drill down to exactly what they need or want within a click or two. You want to be at the end of their rainbow, precisely what they're searching for. Odds are, if you've narrowed your focus well, you won't have many competitors in your space.

Of the talking channel options, podcasting is the most complicated from a technical perspective. It has the highest requirements in terms of quality and consistency. You absolutely can produce it yourself (Stephen's book *Profitable Podcasting* is a step-by-step guide), but each episode is going to require 10 to 15 hours of work, on average. And that's after you do all the setup, which is probably a good 40 to 50 hours at the very least.

When I decided to launch a podcast in 2015, I knew I didn't want to tie up my agency's team with the production. I did the math and decided I was better off hiring professionals who had a level of skill and a singular focus my team would be hard-pressed to match. That decision meant each podcast episode cost me about two hours including inviting the guest, prepping for the interview (or deciding what I want the solocast to be about), doing the interview, and reviewing the show notes once the episode was edited. That's really about it.

When you're producing a weekly show, the time requirement is an important consideration. This is a channel where cutting corners is very evident and will impact your ability to create and grow an audience.

Some of the pros that are unique to podcasting include the co-creation of content. If I do my job right and only allow very smart and generous people on the podcast who have something to teach all of us agency owners, I've just cut my work in half!

Because I know my audience so well—after all, I'm an agency-owner, just like you!—I'm able to craft questions that create many insights and Aha! moments, and trigger much deeper thoughts and ideas. I don't have to be the one with the big ideas, I just have to be the one who knows how to unearth those big ideas and keep digging into them with my guest until I feel all of my audience's questions have been answered.

I don't show up with the answers or insights. I show up with the curiosity and the questions. I'm not saying I don't have to bring value, because I know that I do. I have to be an incredibly good listener and an avid student. I have to be willing to tug on threads I hadn't anticipated (that's the element of improv) and need the ability to guide my guests to their best content.

But I don't have to create it all on my own. I get to borrow other people's smarts, experiences, and expertise and share them with my audience. I am credited with bringing that knowledge to them and making it accessible, tying it to our industry, and asking the very questions the audience wants to ask. That's a huge plus for podcasting. As a host, you don't have to be the sole creator; you can be the curator.

One of the cons of producing podcasts and video series is that their shelf life is limited, so you need to keep creating. Unlike a book, or even a conference presentation, you can't release a new podcast or video episode only whenever you feel like it. People need the consistency of a schedule and a frequency of release that feeds their appetite. Because they're consumed in a relatively short period of time (an hour or less, typically), you've got to keep making more content.

When my agency produces a podcast for a client, we require them to produce six to eight episodes before we publish the first one. Usually, by then, we (and they) can gauge whether or not they have enough gas in their tank to keep producing long-term. That's probably a reasonable test for you, as well.

The equipment costs for producing podcasts and videos can be another con. We're not talking tens of thousands of dollars, but we aren't talking about a mere ten dollars, either. Facebook guru Mari Smith has produced a comprehensive list of equipment that can handle any podcast or video needs, and we highly recommend her advice. Check it out at www.marismith.com/videokit.

The Realities of Video Shows

When it comes to video, the numbers don't lie. The Publicis Media agency Zenith recently released research documenting that globally, consumers watch 84 minutes of video a day, but that includes everything from YouTube to Netflix. The research also showed that video consumption is still on a growth pattern with no signs of stopping.

The good news is that online video content like Netflix is training our consumers to make video consumption a part of their daily habit. The bad news is, it also sets the production bar higher than it's been in a long time. Most brands (and agencies) who are producing a video series are doing some version of run-and-gun or talking-head videos (whether you're walking along a country road or not).

If you aren't ready to produce the next *Game of Thrones*, then it's the content that needs to be above reproach because it is the star of the show.

You have many options in terms of the type of content you want to include in your video series, including:

- explainers
- video blogs (vlogs)
- tutorials
- webinars (more on this in a bit)
- testimonials
- interviews
- live streams/live video

The pros of developing a video channel as your cornerstone are compelling. Distribution on social channels, your own YouTube channels, and other avenues is both easy and typically free. Once the video episode is produced, it's accessible to just about anyone with a single click.

The audience (all of us) is already well-trained and comfortable with the medium, so there's no effort required on your part to educate them on how to get to the goods. According to a study by Insivia, mobile video consumption rises by 100 percent every year, and Hubspot's study showed that 78 percent of people watch online videos every week while 55 percent watch at least one video a day.

One of the most compelling arguments for video is the shareability. Ninety-two percent of users who watch video on their mobile devices will share it with others. With a simple click, they're sharing your message with their circle of influence. (And it goes without saying that if your video isn't high-quality or well-considered, audiences will be unlikely to share it.)

Odds are, because you're sharing these kinds of insights with your clients, you know that video content improves SEO, conversions, and traffic. All good reasons to consider video for your own sales and marketing efforts.

A big pro for video is the size of YouTube's influence on Google searches and its own search volume. If you can define your audience and keywords precisely, video makes you very findable.

But video is not without its challenges, with consumer attention span the biggest among them. Unlike podcasts, which tend to hold an audience for a more extended period of time, video consumers abandon content much more quickly. Anything over a couple of minutes had better be sticky as can be, or else you're going to lose most eyes before your big close. For the majority of us, the most difficult part of this particular issue is delivering enough value with enough concision that we keep our audience's attention. This is an art many struggle to master.

Even for the most confident of professionals, it can be daunting to appear on camera. That fear can paralyze many a potential video host. The only cure for this is jumping in with both feet and shooting some footage. Most people get more comfortable with experience. But if you can't shake the nerves, you might want to reconsider your channel choice. When someone is anxious on camera, they can appear stiff, disinterested, robotic, or awkward. Hardly the way to position yourself as a confident and competent authority!

Obviously, if you're live streaming, you've got to be incredibly comfortable on camera. There are no re-dos or take-twos!

Because of this discomfort and the medium itself, video typically takes a pretty large time investment. Many people create a word-for-word script, which can be time-consuming on its own, and the filming time can expand, as well. Because we're concerned with how we look and sound, many people shoot and re-shoot the same footage many times.

Like podcasting, video editing and production take time and equipment—not huge issues, but worthy of factoring into your consideration. Also, like podcasting, video requires a frequency that allows you to stay connected and continue to add value to your audience on a consistent basis. That adds to the time commitment.

Another con is the abundance of video out there. How do you make yours stand out? How do you fight and win the attention of your audience? You know the answer—a narrow niche and a commitment to providing useful, insightful content that helps members of your audience do their jobs better. Resist that directive, and you'll only create more video noise that gets bypassed because it looks, sounds, and feels like everyone else's.

In our opinion, video works best if you're already seen as an authority at some level. It's tough for someone with no audience, no credibility, and no authority to break through the crowded video space.

An easy-to-solve problem is the fact that most people, between 85 and 90 percent, depending on the study, consume video without the sound on. Think of how and where you consume bite-sized videos like the ones we're talking about here. Odds are you're consuming them on your phone and often in a place that makes the sound inconvenient, if not downright rude. Be sure you add captioning to any videos you produce so your audience doesn't have to wait to consume your content, making it more likely they'll skip it altogether because they're not in a place where they can listen comfortably.

If you're considering a video series that includes interviews, you'll have to decide if you want to physically be in the same place with your guest or do it over a teleconferencing platform like Zoom. Both options present their own opportunities and hurdles.

There's no denying the power and reach of video. It may be the perfect choice for you and your agency.

The Realities of Webinars

Webinars, on the surface, are the homely, less sexy member of the talking cornerstone family. They feel more academic and less showbiz-like. But that doesn't mean they aren't worthy of consideration.

According to research done by Demand Gen Report, 76 percent of B2B buyers have used webinars to make a purchase decision in the last 12 months. The same audience ranks webinars among the top three content types they find most engaging and consume with consistent frequency.

The webinar audience is an interesting one. More than half of the signups don't happen until the week leading up to the event. But don't interpret that as indifference. On average, they will watch a webinar for 57 minutes. That's a huge number when you consider the attention span of an audience today.

One of the biggest pros of creating a webinar channel is that your audience is invested. No one signs up for a webinar if they have no interest in the topic. Note that I didn't say "interested in buying something." If an agency fails the "no selling" rule, it's the most noticeable and offensive in the webinar space. When we, as consumers, think about webinars, we equate them with education, not sales pitches.

Another huge pro for webinars is that they can be easily designed to be evergreen. If you structure the content correctly, you can put your webinars on your website and let people access them at their convenience. Be sure to add the option to download a transcript of the webinar to get all of the Google juice you can.

You don't need any special equipment other than a decent headset to conduct a webinar, which means you can do them live or pre-record them from any location. Subscriptions to any of the webinar platforms are very affordable, and the tools are simple to use.

It gets a little more complicated if you include a guest presenter as part of the webinar's content. You don't have to be in the same place, of course, but your guests probably won't be interested in recording at 2 a.m. or on the weekends, which you might be willing to do.

One of my favorite pros when it comes to webinars is the live element. I like the audience interaction, questions, and engagement. Yes, this means you need to be able to pivot as the conversation flows and maintain control of the crowd, but there's an energy to live presentation that keeps everyone's heads in the game. I also think it's a smart way for audiences to get a sense of who you are and what you're about. They can watch how you interact with both the people you know and the new folks. They get a sense of the relationships you have with your audience, and they can participate, kick your tires, so to speak, in a safe environment that doesn't feel like a sales call. It's a nice combination of learning and hanging out that leaves guests with a sensation somewhere between going to class and having drinks with the professor.

The biggest downside to using the webinar as your cornerstone is that they're much better when people are in the virtual room with you. Which means you first need an audience that would sign up to attend, and you have to promote each webinar to gather that audience. That promotion can fatigue your audience if you're trying to do webinars on a frequency that gives you enough content to break apart into your cobblestones.

Technically, if you're pre-recording the webinar, you don't have to have other people online with you. You can even fake a Q&A session based on the questions you think you'd be asked. But much of the banter and interaction you'd have during a live recording would be missing, of course.

Another potential con for webinars is that they're perceived as the not-so-sexy cousin to podcasting, video, and public speech. Depending on your niche, that may not matter at all, and in fact, it may be a plus. But for others, doing webinars may feel a little old-school.

Don't let this attitude about webinars keep you from considering it as your cornerstone, however. For the right audience, it is absolutely the right choice.

The Realities of Being a Speaker

This is either an exciting possibility for you or a horrifying suggestion. If you fall into the horrified category, just move on to the next chapter. Positioning yourself as an authority in the speaking space, and booking enough gigs so that it becomes your cornerstone, is no easy task. If it's something you're already skittish about, odds are low that you'll do the required heavy lifting.

There's plenty to love about this potential cornerstone. One of the most compelling reasons to consider it is the power of the third-party endorsement. When you're invited to speak at a conference, there's an implied stamp of approval that certifies you as an expert. Several agency owners I know employ this strategy, and they rarely leave a conference or event without an invitation to further engage with a prospect, submit a proposal, or participate in an RFP that is right up their alley. And it's not uncommon that they simply walk away with a new client.

Like webinars, part of the fun of this channel is the audience interaction. It's a rush to have people connecting with you from the stage. There's an intimacy to this particular brand of cornerstone content that's hard to replicate in any of the others. You're a rock star of sorts, and your audience is responding to your music live and in person. If you haven't done a lot of speaking, I think you'll be surprised at how intimate a connection can be, even if you're speaking to a couple thousand people.

You also get real-time feedback on which of your ideas are really resonating. Based on the audience's reactions, questions, and comments during and after your presentation, you'll know which elements of your speech to slice and dice into smaller bits of content. In fact, some agency owners have tested three or four different presentations on live audiences to determine which one to develop more deeply in a book or podcast series. Certainly, you don't have to do either of those things, but as a side benefit, speaking is like hosting your own focus group to gauge the success of these kinds of projects.

Another big plus for speaking as your cornerstone is how high-profile it is. It's easy to market and socially celebrate that you're speaking at a major event. It can become part of your biography or your agency's credibility in a specific space, and speaking instantly positions you as someone noteworthy. "Bob has been fortunate enough to speak at Inbound, TechCrunch's Disrupt, and South by Southwest" has a nice ring to it, but keep in mind, the only stage that should matter to you is the stage that puts you in front of your sweet-spot prospects. For our purposes, I would much rather see your credits say, "Mary is a frequent subject matter expert speaker at shows like World of Concrete, Pacific

Coast Builders Conference, and The Buildings Show," if your niche is some aspect of the construction industry.

What's particularly cool about speaking is that it's easy to brag about, both in the moment and in the past tense. You can share on your agency's Facebook page or in your LinkedIn profile that you're about to speak at an upcoming event. But you can also leverage that speaking gig in your bio or your agency's credibility deck, using video footage of the presentation on your YouTube channel and much more. The exposure and "celebrity" extends far beyond the event's actual audience. You get the credit from not only your live audience, but also anyone who can still understand what your presentation, and the fact that you have presented, says about you as an authority.

Most people would rather die than speak in front of a live audience. So part of the credit you get as a speaker is simply having the courage to open your mouth on a stage! This is an excellent time to remind you that size shouldn't be your ultimate goal. There are plenty of smaller, regional events that need good speakers and have your ideal prospects in the attendee pool. Depending on the size of your agency and your capacity for new clients, smaller events might serve you better. Be careful that your ego doesn't get in the way of you booking profitable speaking opportunities, big or small.

Speaking is one of those cornerstones in which one piece of content often leads to another. If you kill it on one stage, odds are you will get an invitation to another. That said, killing it isn't as easy as it sounds. This is one of the cornerstone channels where presentation and style matter as much as the content itself. It takes years of practice to be a world-class speaker where you are fielding more invitations than you can consider or accept.

For most people who choose this channel, the hustle to book speaking opportunities is definitely a con. There are speaker RFPs to complete, and you need some table stakes tools like a speaker reel video, a speaker one sheet, and some other items. The only way to get a speaker reel is to speak. But most of the really attractive events aren't going to even consider you until you have a reel. Which means you need to speak or pay to record yourself at some smaller venues to earn your way up the food chain, if that's the goal.

This strategy also requires, at a much deeper level than some of the others, a very narrow niche. If you're going to stand out in the sea of marketing speakers, you'd better have a hook. One of the ways I built the authority position for my agency was speaking at banking and credit union conferences for years. We had so much experience and so many examples and case studies, it was hard to argue with our depth of expertise.

Which leads to another misstep that many agency owners make in pursuit of speaking gigs. Choose your audience wisely. Only speak at events where the audience is filled with your prospects. There are many vanity conferences out there with fraternities and sororities of like-minded individuals, where all the cool kids speak, but if you don't believe you can meet a perfect prospect in the audience, just say thank you and decline the invitation. Keep your eye on the prize.

This goes for the keynote, the workshop, and the breakout sessions, too. Depending on the conference, it may better serve you to speak to a smaller subset of the audience in a more intimate setting, a smaller room. As I mentioned before, it's critical that you keep your ego in check if you're going to pursue this channel.

One of the biggest cons for this choice is that you're not in control. Yes, you can record video of every presentation, and you can leverage each opportunity, but if you don't get invited to speak, you don't speak. A dry spell can kill your biz-dev efforts. Which means you have to be a very compelling choice. For speaking to truly be your cornerstone, you need to book a minimum of six events a year. That's when people really begin to peg you as a go-to expert in your field of expertise.

To get to that number, some people might consider speaking for free or for travel expense reimbursement. I know this is going to rub some of you the wrong way. After all, you should get paid for sharing your expertise, right? But there's that dang ego popping its head up. I'm not suggesting what you're talking about isn't providing value. But for you, the real value exchange isn't in a speaking fee, but in the exposure to your sweet-spot audience and the endorsement of the conference which will automatically elevate the audience's perception of your depth of expertise and authority.

Think of it this way. What would you pay for the opportunity to be put in front of a room of a hundred ideal prospects? You would be introduced and positioned as an expert, you would get to share your insights for about 45 minutes to demonstrate your knowledge, and at the end, you could collect all of your attendees' names and contact information so you could follow up. On top of all that, you would get a video of your presentation for promotional purposes, and you could tell the world you were chosen to speak to this particular audience. Seriously, what would you pay? Most of you would pay a pretty penny. So stop whining about not getting paid to speak. The real payday is far beyond a single speaker's fee. Don't get me wrong, if you can get paid, that's lovely. But this doesn't have to be an immediate revenue generator to have an incredible ROI.

Another con to this option of cornerstone content is that it requires a great deal of time. From chasing after opportunities to prepping your presentation to the actual travel to and from the event, you're going to invest a lot of your time in this effort. There are no shortcuts here.

For most of you, speaking may be a better cobblestone than cornerstone. If you develop your cornerstone content well, it's easy to see how you might get invited to speak at a relevant trade show once or twice a year. Whether your cornerstone content is a book, a podcast, or research, as it garners attention it can easily lead to a handful of speaking opportunities. Those opportunities will expose new people to your cornerstone content (serving as a good cobblestone) and significantly reduce the amount of time this channel requires. Being sought out as a speaker rather than having to ferret out the possibilities and compete to win a spot, is a very attractive option, so this isn't an all-or-nothing choice.

If you choose any of the speaking options as your cornerstone, you'll need to be quick on your feet, comfortable speaking with little to no prep, and confident you can demonstrate your expertise in any situation. Even if you've studied and rehearsed your presentation, you're never 100 percent in control at any event. Above all else, you need to be ready for the live audience to take your efforts in a different direction than you might have intended. One oddball question or comment can quickly send you into waters you hadn't anticipated. Handling such circumstances with grace while maintaining your authority position isn't easy, but if you're wired to be in the spotlight, it can be both intoxicating and profitable!

Chapter Eight: Writing as the Hub of Your Cornerstone Content

(Stephen)

Chapter Seven drilled into cornerstone content that will help you be heard. Now we're going to give you the upside of being found through written cornerstone content. We will also address some of the potential disadvantages to the various written content formats.

We will focus our discussion on your agency's blog, articles, books, and research projects. Let's start with the overarching pros and cons of written cornerstone content.

PROs

- You can rewrite—you aren't doing this work in front of an audience.

- You can create this content without any special equipment or additional expense.

- You can create this content at 2 a.m. on a remote island—anywhere, at any time.

- If you have co-creators, you get to promote on their channels, too.

- Your audience can consume the content on the go.

- You get to control the length of the content.

- You get to control the frequency of publication.

- There's lots of SEO value, especially in blog posts and articles.

- With the exception of books, written work is easy and instantaneous to share on social media.

CONs

- You can easily get caught in perfectionism paralysis.

- You have to be a good writer or have an amazing editor.

- The time commitment, especially for a book, can be significant.

- If you're thinking articles or blog posts, it's not a one-and-done channel. You have to keep producing to create a body of work.

- If it's badly written, it speaks volumes about your agency's capabilities.

- Typos and grammatical errors are much easier to spot in written formats.

- You have fewer options if you want to deploy the Trojan horse of sales.

- You aren't taking advantage of two of the hottest trends of our time, voice and video.

The Realities of Blogging

Blogging has been a staple for many agencies for over a decade. Granted, most agency blogs gather dust like that treadmill in your spare bedroom, but for the agencies that actually created consistent content and actually shared their expertise as we've discussed in previous chapters, they've enjoyed the SEO boost and cumulative effect of their helpful content.

But the problem is most blog posts found on most agency websites are generic and incorrectly optimized for search. The context of the content isn't designed to answer the questions your audience is asking, or drive search traffic to your site. And that means most blogs aren't delivering a lot of value to the audience or the agency. But with a new understanding and mindset, that's easy to shift to. If your agency was to develop a more provocative point of view, or you routinely taught your subject matter from the platform as an expert, or you considered opening up your blog to guest contributors to increase the frequency of your posts from once a month to perhaps daily, then blogging could grow into a very smart and effective cornerstone channel.

With a popular blog that ranks well in search engine results using keywords that tie to your niche, you will drive organic traffic to your website. And not just any, but high-quality traffic, filled with potential prospects for your shop. Not only will that serve you well from a biz-dev aspect, but having a consistent flow of visitors also means your blog is a media channel you can monetize through other people seeking to connect to your audience. You can sell a sponsorship or ads to brands who want to communicate with the narrow niche of people who read your content. To get serious, you first need to get strategic about your editorial calendar in terms of specific blog topics, writing assignments, and themes you want to build into your content. This will help you avoid last-minute panic when you're approaching your publication deadline, which often results in either a less-than-ideal blog post or a lapse in posting altogether.

An efficient way to goose up your blog's volume and value is to invite other non-competing experts to share their knowledge on your site. Go to the biggest trade show for your niche and walk the exhibit floor. Pick up the business cards of all the vendors in attendance and invite them to submit content. You'll need strict no-solicitation rules and to edit the content carefully to make sure it's delivering on your value proposition, but eight times out of ten, you'll get some very useful content that aligns well with what you're writing. Be careful with this strategy—you don't want to use so much guest content that your voice becomes muffled—but if you want to become a knowledge hub for your target audience, this is a powerful and efficient way to make that happen.

There are a few downsides to going all-in on your blog as your cornerstone. If you were reading this book in 2006, it would have probably been our strongest recommendation. But since that time, billions of blog posts have been published online. It's challenging to be found in such a crowded space. If you want to blog as your cornerstone, you need to be prepared to produce a significant amount of content and publish several times a week. It's the only way to make a dent.

Another con to blogging is that you may miss out on the explosive growth taking place in audio content right now. Modern technology makes it simple to interact with a virtual assistant like Alexa or Siri while you're cooking dinner or to listen to a podcast while you're on the treadmill. Audio formats are on a huge growth curve and will likely continue to grow for years to come.

Don't discount turning your written blogs into audio content. Short-form podcasts, Alexa flash briefings, or other audio outlets are certainly a possibility. You can turn that con into a pro pretty quickly.

The Realities of Writing Articles

In spite of the chant that print is dead, magazines are enjoying a huge resurgence. Not only have mainstream publications like *Forbes*, *Entrepreneur*, and *Inc.* upped their game, but niche publications are flourishing these days by offering a combination of print and online products. So don't dismiss this channel as merely a 1990s option; it's relevant and powerful even now.

Furthermore, writing articles for trade publications you know your target audience reads religiously can offer a steady stream of exposure to your niche, giving you credibility. It's easy to get intoxicated by the prestige of titles like *Fast Company*, but don't overlook the opportunity to get picked up by target publications that serve your core audience. The audience might be small but spot-on for your counsel and point of view.

The credibility that comes with being consistently featured in top-tier publications may also attract invitations for you to speak at industry events or opportunities to collaborate with partners and joint ventures, all of which will raise awareness for your agency and build more opportunities to monetize your content. Depending on the publication, if your content is spot-on for their audience, you may garner an invitation to be a regular contributor or columnist, which will provide consistent, high-quality inbound links back to your agency's website, give you an impressive title to include in your bio, elevate the credibility of your expertise, and assist with your search engine optimization.

There are also a few disadvantages to using articles as your cornerstone content. The big one is that, as it is with public speaking, you have little control or influence over the distribution of that content. You could provide an editor with an article, and they may ask you to make several rounds of revisions or because you're not the only one trying to leverage this strategy, it may take eight to 10 weeks to get your article posted just because there's a long queue of content in the system, and that's if they decide to publish it at all.

They have a right to modify your content as well. You can always opt out at that point, but demanding that they publish your article exactly how you submitted it is rarely an option. Even if you do get your article accepted and you are fine with the editorial changes, it's unlikely you'll be permitted to include any sort of call-to-action within your author byline. While it's very cool to be able to say you wrote something for one of these well-known publications, or the leading trade publication in your field of expertise, using articles as your cornerstone is a more passive option and much harder to influence and control.

The Realities of Writing a Book

Given that you're reading a book that we wrote, you might surmise we are big fans of authoring a book as a cornerstone channel. No doubt about it, it comes with some pretty significant pros. It's tough to find another channel that can surpass the credibility of you being the author of an industry-centric book or books. Nearly every highly paid professional speaker has written at least one book. There is an age-old saying that goes like this: "Talkers are hawkers, but writers are experts." You can see there's a lot of truth to this in how the marketplace reacts to authors. Even today, with all the self-publishing options out there, authors garner more respect than speakers, as it has always been. Time will tell if that changes, but for now, it's still a solid truth. Writing a book gives you the opportunity to firmly plant your flag, and to do it at a depth that other forms of content cannot match in the minds of your target audience. The written word has great power. It has been woven into our DNA for millennia. And let's face it—coming up with a hundred or 200 pages or more of content is no small task, so it makes sense that the effort earns ample respect.

Writing a book will immediately elevate you to the status of expert in your field. It will also put you into a rare category as an agency owner. There just aren't that many agency owners who have invested the time and effort it takes to become a book author. Your book, if nothing else, will act as a unique 3-D business card for your agency. Doors will open for speaking engagements and conference presentations. You will no longer be seen as the agency owner who wants to attend a conference to walk the exhibit hall for prospects. No, your prospects are coming to hear you deliver the keynote because of the research you've done, who you interviewed for your book, and the trends you unveiled as a result of your work. It completely shifts everyone's perspective.

Authoring a book that is narrow in focus around your area of expertise will also open you up to reviews, interviews, and social media shares. Journalists will reach out to you on Twitter and ask you to comment on something for an article they're writing. Podcast hosts will reach out to you on LinkedIn and ask you to be a guest on their shows. You will become a celebrity in your niche because you had the daily discipline to get it done.

Writing a book also provides you with a tremendous number of slicing and dicing opportunities, as you can imagine. A 150-page book can easily feed your cobblestone channels for a year or more.

As you might have guessed, the big con to writing a book is that it takes a significant time investment. Even writing a bad book takes a lot of time and effort. But writing a book that is truly valuable and serves your prospects so they can be better at their jobs? That takes some serious time and effort. There are many unfinished manuscripts sitting on agency owner's laptops, I'm sure. There are many tips and hacks for making it happen, but they're all about gaming your calendar or keeping yourself psyched up when you're tired of getting up at 5 a.m. to carve out a couple hours of writing.

You can definitely find ways to make the task of writing a book easier and more doable. But no hack or tip can make it happen quickly or effortlessly. The perks of this channel are huge because they're hard-earned.

If you decide this is the channel for you, take control of your schedule, get the hard work done, and revel in the upside. The authority positioning and the biz-dev boost for your agency is significant.

The good news is that you only need to write a book every few years to be considered prolific. Who knows, you might find it so gratifying, the heavy lifting is something you just build into your routine.

The Realities of Conducting Research

If credibility is what you're after, then commissioning a bona fide research project that serves your agency's niche can definitely deliver the goods. A research study can uniquely reinforce or validate your point of view, and you will achieve significant distinction from competing agencies. Very few agencies have the technical prowess or partnerships in place to conduct statistically valid research. We're not talking a quick SurveyMonkey effort here. We mean partnering up with a researcher and doing it correctly and well.

When you have statistically valid data *and* insights from that data, your prospects, existing clients, and the media will all clamor to learn more. In today's world of hyperbole, fake news, and Insta-celebrities, people are hungry for facts and data. Because of the pace of change, we also love data that suggests trends or patterns we can use to our advantage. The insights you gain from your own research are evergreen, and you will refer to past studies for years to come, building a library of knowledge as you do more studies over time.

If you decide to head down the path of conducting research, don't be surprised if a third-party brand reaches out to sponsor your work. If you've stayed true to your niche, there will be other companies who also want to connect with your defined audience. Several of the agencies we know who conduct primary research have a partner who covers all of the hard costs in exchange for a sponsorship position.

Now, there are definitely some disadvantages to research projects. First, we would highly encourage you to work with an experienced and qualified research partner who can help you elevate the project with their careful creation of the research instrument and their professional prowess in interpreting the data collected. That comes with a price tag, but when you compare that upfront cost to the profits you will earn from the first clients the research brings to your door, it's easy to justify. It's a little like the down-payment on your first house. You know it's totally worth it, but it still stings to write the check.

Another con to using research as your cornerstone channel is that it's not instantaneous. It's going to take a few months to decide on a focus area, develop the research tool, conduct the research, and analyze the results. You'll need to plan in advance if you want to use this as the hub of your efforts.

Depending on your personality, another consideration may be a pro or a con. Even though much of the research is handled through writing, including the results documents, executive summaries, etc., you're going to end up talking about the data as well. Whether it's on a conference stage, a podcast, or some other form of interview, the value of doing the research is that the insights you'll discover will open up many new doors. Some of them will put you in the spotlight, so you'll have to decide if that makes this option better or worse.

No matter which direction you go—talking or writing—remember, your decision is never written in stone. It's very important, but never permanent. Also, there isn't one right answer. Several options could probably work perfectly for your sweet-spot prospects. Start small and focused. Experiment.

Your cornerstone content needs to be meaty enough that it can generate a significant number of cobblestones, but any of the options we've presented will do that. Don't let making this decision derail your efforts or stall you and your team's enthusiasm. You can make adjustments as you go, but for now, pick a channel that will serve as your hub, and let's talk about what you can do with it!

Chapter Nine: Extending your Reach and ROI

(Stephen)

Extensions. Earlier in the book, we talked about finding multiple ways to use and monetize your content. The obvious way to monetize your content (and for most agencies, the biggest and most important) is to use content as your biz-dev driver. But there are plenty of other ways. When you build out your content, attract and delight a community, and stay focused on helping your audience get better at their jobs every day, you create multiple opportunities.

The first set of opportunities involves a direct revenue stream, meaning you're getting paid in exchange for something you sell, do, share, teach, etc. This could be a webinar series, an online course, software as a service, live events, remote or digital events, coaching or training sessions, a tool kit, templates, etc., and that's just scratching the surface.

Through the direct revenue model, your audience buys you and your agency's smarts in a variety of formats.

The indirect model becomes an option after you have established a large enough community that you can sell access to this community to third parties. Think sponsorships, digital ads, and the like. You're not delivering any additional content or service. You're simply selling someone exposure to your audience.

Typically, your cornerstone or hub's popularity will allow you to create spokes you can use to generate revenue. An easy example is a live event. This is 100 percent optional, and entirely your call. Some agency owners don't want to charge for events they host because it's all part of their new business strategy, and for them, it's about the attendance and the numbers. Others want to diversify how their agency makes money, and the extensions mentioned above are a smart way to do that. We can think through this scenario with a simple choice. Ask yourself, "Do I want to plant seeds to harvest later, or pick what's growing now?"

In my agency, for more than five years, we hosted monthly morning events we called "branding breakfasts." We held them at what I consider an ungodly hour, 7:30 a.m., and as people came in and chatted, we offered a simple hot breakfast. Our goal was to combine networking with conversation about branding, which was one of our core offerings. People would come in, sit down, have breakfast, and chat. Near the end of breakfast, as the guests were wrapping up, I would do a 20 to 30-minute presentation. I would choose some very focused aspect of branding like "How do we know when it's time to refresh our logo?" and present it to the group. We'd do some Q&A and group discussion, and everyone would be on their merry way by 8:30 or 9 a.m. We didn't charge attendees, but they did have to make a reservation. If they no-showed, they owed us $15 for the breakfast.

For us, these events served multiple purposes. Primarily, they were about lead-generation and establishing our expertise. It also forced me to create new content about branding every month. We'd turn the PowerPoint deck into a SlideShare file, and I'd use the same content in my column and the blog. It was also an easy way for us to help smaller companies and non-profits that couldn't afford to hire us. It was a mix of biz-dev, content development, and community goodwill. That worked for me. I thought of it as a sampling experience, not unlike how people go to Costco to wander around the store and get a free lunch. Sooner or later, they end up buying some of the items they tasted, and we certainly experienced that as well. By helping our attendees be smarter at their jobs, we earned a significant amount of new business, and some of those clients are still with us today.

The breakfasts were quite popular, and we'd routinely have anywhere from 25 to 40 people there. We'd still be doing it today were it not for the early start. I really, really hate early mornings. When we tried moving it to lunch, our attendance just wasn't significant enough to keep going. And I was over the 7:30 a.m. thing. So we just wound them down. That was probably 10 or more years ago, and we still get referrals from attendees today. It was a fantastic seed-planting strategy.

Another way we have built out extensions in my shop is through developing curriculum. We were hired by a national association to develop a two-day social media workshop for non-profit organizations to offer to their members for continuing education credits. We got paid two ways through a fee for developing the course and a revenue share of the registration fees.

We eventually offered this course through four different national associations. We swapped out the examples to tailor the materials to their membership's makeup, but the core content was the same.

We developed, delivered, modified, and re-delivered that content for several years, and it easily generated six figures of "side hustle" income each year. We also scored two clients and several referrals from the attendees, simply by doing these continuing education (CE) events.

A twist on this idea is what AMI agency Marshall Communications, based in Maine, does. They hold social media boot camps. They travel to different cities in their region and teach half-day primers on social media best practices. They get local chambers, banks, and other businesses to sponsor these events. The agency makes the revenue, and the sponsor gets to invite whoever they'd like to the event. Then the two entities (sponsor and agency) co-promote the event to draw in even more people.

Naturally, the intention is the immediate revenue, but it's also an opportunity for content creation, social media sharing, and business development.

Another way agencies are using events to create revenue is by partnering with Google, Facebook, or their local media vendors to host trends events. We've had many AMI agencies who have a big enough spend with Google or Facebook that these major companies will cover the entire cost of the event, including fees for guest speakers. Then, the agencies promote the event. They can choose to sell tickets or give them away. We have agencies big and very small employ this strategy, and it works like a charm for both. These events have been held in major markets and tiny little towns. Again, all with a huge ROI for the agencies.

One of our agencies, Five Stones Media out of Hammond, La., did something super smart when they brought Google in. They sold additional sponsorships to local businesses, who got a specific number of tickets based on their sponsorship level. Every one of those sponsors had their own list, so the promotion of the event was easily magnified.

Five Stones also did a pre-event drawing and offered a handful of the attendees an assessment of their digital presence right after the event ended. That opportunity generated a ton of interest and biz-dev activity for them.

Another AMI agency is infamous for its pre-tradeshow cocktail parties. They secure a couple of the conference's speakers to attend, then they invite their clients and best prospects, billing the event as an opportunity to rub elbows in an intimate setting with some big movers and shakers.

Your event extension doesn't have to even have a defined business focus. AMI agency AOR out of Denver throws a blow-out annual party in their office every summer. People are asking for the dates of the party six months in advance because they want to plan around it! Naturally, they have samples of their work throughout the office, and there's plenty of business that gets done, despite the party atmosphere.

All of these events are also smart PR opportunities, depending on the event and the audience. It might be your local business journal or daily paper. It might be a trade publication or a local TV station. The ROI on these events can be multi-fold and have a very long tail.

Though they lack sex appeal, webinars are incredibly popular and effective, as we talked about in Chapter Seven. For a small percentage of agencies, webinars could make the best cornerstone content. But for most, they're going to be cobblestones, which means you should think about whether you can monetize them. In many cases, it can be that initial purchase that leads to more investment in your services down the line.

It's a very versatile channel. You can do webinars in any cadence, length, or on any sub-topic within your niche and POV. You can record them live, with participants present, or pre-record them and seed in questions throughout, or you can host them live and then use the recording as an evergreen resource.

If you don't want to monetize them, they are at the very least great content for your website or YouTube channel. If you're using them on your site, be sure you transcribe them so search engines can drive people to you. If you do want to monetize them, think about a subscription service model where your buying public can access a library of webinars (some already recorded and some scheduled to be recorded) and view them on demand.

Beyond the potential revenue, if you decide to go this route, webinars are a great way to give some of your more junior team members an opportunity to hone their speaking skills. It's a little less intimidating than standing in front of a live crowd, and you or they can test ideas with a live audience you might want to use in your cornerstone channel down the road.

If you are going to charge for your webinars, remember that 99 percent of them out there are free. You might need to add some more sizzle to attract buyers. Some agencies offer a 30-minute consultation in conjunction with completing the webinar, or some other additional value.

In terms of pricing, we've seen success everywhere from $9 to $499! It's all about the value proposition. If you want a large crowd, selling access might not be the best route. But if you'd rather have a smaller audience of buyers with serious intentions or challenges, why not test their interest with a fee?

Email-based mini-courses are another effective extension. Again, this would be a hyper-focused aspect of what you specialize in, your niche, that also introduces the audience to your point of view if it makes sense within the context of the course. Typically, these stretch out for a week or a few weeks, depending on how much homework is required in between each email.

We've had a couple AMI member PR agencies create mini-courses on crisis communication planning. (They didn't do them together, they just both picked the same topic.) Each lesson of the course taught a specific aspect of creating a crisis communication plan, like putting together an emergency communication tree so that all interested parties are kept in the loop. In one case, the agency also created a private Facebook group for the participants.

I can hear some of you asking, "Why give it away for free when you can sell it?" Both courses really took people through the steps and stages that the client would have needed to do on their own, even if they'd hired the agency to develop the overall plan. There was very little room for revenue in those activities. But what it did was establish the depth of expertise these agencies had in this deliverable. Both have earned multiple clients from the effort.

If you want to take the mini-course idea to the next level, you could develop online training courses. An AMI agency that focuses on clients in the knitting and crafts industries found that they were getting a lot of inquiries from companies that couldn't afford them. They didn't want to turn their backs on these businesses, so they built an industry-specific Marketing 101 course online. They were able to offer that as an alternative to simply saying no thank you to those little prospects. I don't think they did, but this would have been a great sponsorship opportunity for an industry-specific association or tradeshow.

For many agencies, public speaking is an extension. Few will choose to make it their cornerstone, but many will speak a couple of times a year, monetize their presentations as biz-dev opportunities, and in some cases, also get paid to speak.

What ties all of these extension opportunities together is that they are born from a strong hub or cornerstone that has attracted an audience and transformed them into a community of fans. When someone loves your content, and you have genuinely helped them get better at their job, they get hungry for more. You can generate revenue in several ways from selling access to the extension itself to selling access to the audience consuming the extension's content. Beyond that, even if you give it all away for free, it will lead to referrals and new business opportunities.

As you build out your master plan, be mindful of how important and profitable extensions can be!

Chapter Ten: Your New Business Blueprint

(Drew)

One of the most erroneous statements made about authority marketing is that it only serves the top of your sales funnel. We could not disagree more.

Yes, if you only produce random pieces of content and push that content out on social channels, it may be accurate, but you aren't going to do that. In this chapter, we'll demonstrate how your authority position can provide incredible value for your prospects throughout their entire buyer's journey, whether that takes a day or a decade.

When I'm working with an agency, and we map out their sales funnel, there are typically some gaping holes in the funnel, which means there's no easy way for the prospect to move from one section of the funnel into another. That's the job of your cobblestones. To provide a simple and attractive path that ultimately leads your prospect toward feeling ready to buy.

Let's look at the different phases of every agency's sales funnel and demonstrate how this might work. There are four distinct phases I've named—the macro, micro, nano, and existing clients in every sales funnel. It's worth noting that while we talk about the sales funnel like it's linear, it's most certainly not. Prospects can move back and forth within the funnel, swimming both up and downstream repeatedly. But for our purposes, it's easier to be simplistic. Sooner or later, you need your prospects to move through all of the phases and get to the buying stage, no matter how many times they bounce back and forth before they get there.

For what feels like eons, on the agency side of my world, I have used the "know–like–trust trilogy" to help prospects and clients understand the buyer's journey. It's no accident that these align perfectly with the macro, micro, and nano phases.

The macro phase aligns with "know." This is the very top of your funnel. Odds are, your prospects have no idea you even exist. They don't know about you. These are people who've never heard of your agency, have no idea who you are, and may not even be looking for an agency at all. They may not even know they have a need, but they're out there. Your whole job in this phase of the sales funnel is to get on their radar. This is where your cornerstone content is king. The prospect is poking around the book store and stumbles upon your book. Or they Google something, and your research report appears in the results. Maybe the prospect is looking for a new podcast for a long drive, and voila! There's your podcast, waiting for them. Or they attend a trade show, and you're a breakout speaker with a topic that interests them enough to wander into your session. Maybe you're writing a column for a trade show pub that's in one of your verticals.

Whatever the specifics, this is the part where you're demonstrating your authority position, and your potential client discovers you. Your content is useful and insightful, so they pay attention. Or maybe the first few times they run across your content, they don't pay any attention, as painful as that is to hear. But sooner or later, they start consuming it and finding value in it, which leads to them wanting more from you. If your content isn't living on your website, odds are they'll go looking for you and ideally, get to your site. This is when you want to offer them several opportunities to self-identify. At this moment, your relationship is very one-sided. They know who you are, but you don't know them. You want to fix that by having tasty offerings (not just a "Contact Us" page or invitations to "Subscribe to Our Newsletter") that they will want badly enough to trade their personal information for—typically an email address.

You can see why your cornerstone content has to be dense in value. It has to be hearty enough to earn a potential client's initial attention and be substantial enough that it nourishes them in a big way. They need to be able to feed off of it until they're ready to step out of the shadows and let you see them. They know that's risky because experience has taught them that it's highly likely that you're going to start bombarding them with sales emails or start calling them. No one is excited about that.

Think of your prospects as a herd of deer you'd like to lure into your yard. Eventually, you want them to eat right out of your hand. At the very first sight of them on the edge of the forest, you wouldn't go running towards them, expecting them to stand there and wait for you. You know they'd bolt at the first sign of your approach. You need to be patient and generous enough to slowly convince them to trust you. You have to let them step toward you, not the other way around. We humans react very much like this herd of deer.

This is one of the most difficult aspects of what we're teaching in this book. You must be patient and resist that gnawing need to chase after and sell clients. You must be confident that your smarts will win them over eventually, and that they will come to you. Later in the book, we'll introduce you to some agencies that demonstrate this discipline and patience, and you will see the rewards that came from that.

The mantra of this entire sales process is, "How can I help my prospects be better at their job today?" Any time you're about to do anything—publish, send, or whatever—ask yourself that question. If what you're about to post or publish can't answer that question, then don't do it. This sounds simplistic, but it's incredibly difficult. I have watched many agency owners violate this rule to the disastrous results you'd expect. It negates everything you'd done to build your authority position.

A true authority doesn't have to chase after business. Business comes to them. This is definitely a "fake it till you make it" situation. Whether you have genuinely earned your authority position or not, you cannot violate this rule. Chasing after clients reeks of desperation. And authorities don't need to be desperate.

Okay, so you've enticed the deer by spreading a generous supply of alfalfa, acorns, and woody browse along the edge of the forest. You do it consistently enough or put out such a large volume of it that they can feed on it for several days. They now know this is a good spot to get nutritious food that sustains them. They are deep in the macro phase. They know this spot and you, the person managing it, and find incredible value in both.

Now they're ready to move a few steps closer because you've put out even more food a bit beyond the forest's edge. They are ready to enter into our micro stage. This is when they have some awareness of you, and their initial impression was a good one. They know who you are. You're on their radar. You might have their email address. You might have their name. They might have thrown their business card into a hat for a drawing when you were speaking at a conference. You have some tangential connection to them, but you don't really have a relationship. This phase is where you begin to build it.

The micro phase is where you create both credibility and connection. For agency prospects, this can also be a very frustrating stage. You can have someone on your email list, clicking on links and drilling down deeper into your content every week, and yet, nothing happens. No call, no completed contact form. Prospects can stay in this phase of the sales cycle for a day or a decade, and there is no predicting which. There are many reasons for their hesitation or stagnation. They might not be in a position to make the buying decision (but someday they will), or they might be in the middle of a contract and don't want to initiate contact until it's closer to when they plan to send out the RFP. They might not even be thinking about hiring an agency—yet. Whatever the reason, leave them be.

The annoying truth is that there's absolutely nothing we can do or offer as an agency to entice someone to buy before they're ready. There is no BOGO offer. No coupon. No limited-time sale. We are a considered purchase, and they will make that purchase when the need is acute enough to do so, not a minute before.

Every week, I have a conversation with an agency owner who talks about purging these people from their list. I am not a fan. There's no harm in you continuing to provide value for as long as it takes for them to be ready.

In the micro stage of the funnel, we are slicing and dicing our cornerstone content and creating all kinds of cobblestones. We are scattering content around, in different places and formats. Let's say your cornerstone content is an annual research project. Here are some examples of how you might take that one piece of content (the research results) and create a variety of cobblestones.

- Each question or result could be a blog post, an infographic, a short video, or a quote card.

- You could appear on other people's podcasts to talk about the results and make some recommendations.

- You could create a series of tweets about specific results.

- You could create a webinar or webinar series on the results. Record it live, then have it available on your website.

You can see how, even within that shortlist, you could easily create a new piece of content every week, if not more often. You could easily have four to six medium-sized (in value, not in dimension) cobblestones that you could promote and share with smaller cobblestones in between. But this doesn't all have to be digital. Your agency might hold an event in your market or tie it to a trade show or some other venue or function where you're offering your expertise and knowledge.

This might also be the phase where testimonials are part of your content strategy. Having someone else say you're good at what you do can be very reassuring. Think of your case studies on the website as another cobblestone. Be sure to ask yourself what a prospect could learn from this case study and apply to their world. Remember our mantra—"How can I help my prospects be better at their job today?"

Now we're moving our audience from knowing that we exist to

actually liking us, getting a sense of our personality, and deciding what it might be like to work with us. We are beginning to create a little bit of relationship at this stage. Granted, it's still at arm's length, but they might start to follow you on social media or even email you with a question. This is the phase where most agencies drop the ball. They'll go to the Herculean effort of creating the cornerstone content, but they cannot sustain the effort of maintaining contact with audiences pre-sale. This is where the magic happens. This is where you're so consistently helpful that the deer are willing to take a few steps into the light, rather than staying invisible inside the forest. But consistency is key. That's what builds the credibility and earns their sense of connection.

One of my favorite aspects of the *Build A Better Agency* podcast is that when I get an email from a reader or meet them at a conference or AMI workshop, they almost always say some variation of, "I feel like I already know you and you're a long-time friend because of how much time we've spent together." That is humbling and gratifying beyond words. And, if I am being 100 percent candid, it also shortens the sales cycle significantly. Which isn't half bad, either.

This phase is about nurturing the lead and getting permission to stay in front of them. As long as you are helpful and useful to them, they will give you permission to stay in touch. You have no idea what day, what week, what month it will be when all of a sudden, this prospect who's been on your list for a while is suddenly going to need an agency. You want to be present and top of mind all the time so that on the day they have the need, you at least get the opportunity to have that conversation. That's what you're trying to do in the micro phase—earn the opportunity to be invited to the table when the client is finally ready.

Back to my deer analogy for a minute. In the micro phase, you keep putting out feed. And without the deer even realizing it, they're moving closer and closer to you each time they consume what you've left for them. Now they know that you exist, and they appreciate, even enjoy, what you're doing for them. Even then, it's still not the time to go running at them. They will still flee back to the protection of the forest. If you thought it required discipline and patience not to run at them during the macro phase, it's 10 times as difficult in the micro phase. But you don't want to spook them when they're so close.

The micro phase of your sales funnel is never-ending. You just keep moving the feed closer and closer until the day the deer will move from like to trust and be willing to be entirely out in the open and slowly and tentatively approach you, eating directly from your outstretched hand.

I can hear what you're thinking: "My God, man! This could take forever! I need some new clients! I can't wait for these skittish deer to take years to eat from my hand!" That's what the nano phase of the sales funnel is all about. It's the accelerant.

The nano section of the sales funnel is where you get very specific about your audience, and you ramp up the effort. That's why you can't have more than 25 prospects at a time in this phase. I don't care how big your agency is or how many people you have working on biz-dev; for this to work, it requires persistence and personalization, and no agency can do it well for more than 25 of your hottest prospects.

These 25 prospects should absolutely fit your best client profile. They should be in the center of your sweet spot. These are prospects you know you can delight, whose world you can rock and who are going to be very profitable for your agency. These are organizations you know would be killer clients for your shop. Create a database of these ideal prospects, and brainstorm highly valuable content you can share with them every six to eight weeks. This content needs to be a mix of online and offline offerings, but they don't all have to be sourced from your agency. Most should, but not all.

This shouldn't be content anyone could find on your website or in other places, but content that makes the potential client feel special and is personalized to them. Any time you can, send this content via snail mail. Even if you could send a PDF of your e-book, for example, print it out on nice paper and mail it in a 9-by-12 envelope. Why? What's the traffic comparison between your inbox and your mailbox? I'm sure you use email far more often, which makes materials sent through snail mail stand out that much more. If you want to get noticed, go to the extra effort and expense. Again, this is why we're only targeting 25 prospects.

We are still honoring our mantra, "How can I help my prospects be better at their job today?" We aren't sending them a capabilities deck about the agency. We aren't pitching their business. We're still leaning on our authority to move them through the stages of know, like, and trust.

Some of the specific things I've seen agencies include in this effort range from a checklist on 10 things to make a TV interview go well (from clothing to soundbite prep) to a list of tradeshow booth ideas to a best-selling business book with a business card tucked in between the pages and a note that says something like, "Hey Babette, I think Chapter Two of this book is particularly pertinent to your organization, considering how quickly you are opening new locations. Hope you find it insightful." That's it. No, "Let's get together to talk about it," or, "We can help you with those location openings." Just the effort to be helpful and make them smarter.

Some of this content can absolutely be cobblestones from your cornerstone content. But now you're also mixing in your business and how you help clients every day, as in the case of the interview tip sheet.

Be sure you think beyond printed content. You might invite them to an educational webinar you're hosting or a lunch-and-learn at your office. You might bring in a subject matter speaker in your niche industry that complements the work you do, like an HR/recruiting specialist in the niche. Maybe you're hosting a pre-tradeshow cocktail party with one of the speakers. Or your research results unveiling event. You get the idea.

Every single thing you send should answer the question, "How can I help my prospects be better at their job today?" It should also be personalized with a handwritten note from you and be spot-on in terms of its targeting.

To make this happen, you need to plan. Do not wait until week seven and say to your team, "Oh, crap! We forgot we need to send a mailer to our nano list next week. What should we send them?" If you do that, either you'll realize you can't come up with something of a high enough value in time, and you destroy the cadence and consistency of the program, or you send them something mediocre and deteriorate any trust you've created.

Have a list of at least 12 to 20 touchpoints and always have the next three to four done and in the can. This is not inexpensive in terms of your time or hard costs. Don't waste the effort by not planning ahead.

Once you start, keep on it. For as long as it takes. Don't take someone off the nano list until one of two things happens—either they hire you, or they get a restraining order and tell you to go away. Otherwise, keep working that list because the reality is, if you've built that list wisely, and you consistently deliver on the plan's goals, you'll get hired by one or two of them a year. And that will result (with all of the other things we're talking about) in a very full and robust pipeline that sustains and grows your agency, year over year.

What happens when you do get hired by one of the companies on the list? You fill in the now-empty slot with another prospect. You keep working that list of 25.

If you mind those three sales funnels, macro, micro, and nano, you're going to encourage many of your prospects to give you the opportunity to win their business. Our world is set up according to a law of averages. The more invitations, the more wins.

But there is a fourth part of the sales funnel. This is the area where most agencies forget about developing their new business strategies. Your existing clients. These are the deer who are already eating out of your hand. They trust you. They value you. Why would we stop wooing them?

Remember that about 70 percent of your net new revenue every year should come from existing clients. It makes perfect sense; they're already giving you money. They're already experiencing the amazing results your shop delivers. Why wouldn't they want to hire you to do more work for them?

You need to have a new business program and a plan aimed at your clients. I'm hoping you all do annual reviews and planning with your clients. What I'm talking about is still staying focused on the question, "How can I help my clients be better at their job today?"

They're going to see you creating all of this content and sharing it with the world. It's human nature to be annoyed that others are getting it for free when they're paying you money. It's like when you get the mailer from your cable company talking about some incredible offer, but when you call about it, you're told it's for new customers only.

Same thing here. You need to do some client-only offerings that make them feel special and valued. You want being a client of your agency to feel like being a part of an insider's club. They should get access to things no one else gets.

You might have a client-only event and bring in a speaker or present some results from your most recent research that you plan to hold back from the public. You might create a client-only email that gives them the scoop on some essential industry information. You get the idea—make them proud to be a member of the club and feel like they get special privileges for doing so. You can probably make this effort two or three times a year if they're rather grand gestures, or if it's mostly along the lines of an "eyes-only" secret info email, once a month.

At the end of the day, we need to be asking ourselves these questions:

- Are we making sure people know who the agency is and where our depth of expertise lies?
- Are we making sure they like the agency because we're being helpful, useful, and demonstrating our knowledge in a way that makes them better at their job?
- Are we doing this consistently enough that they trust us with their business?
- And once we have earned their trust and their business, what are we doing to retain them?

It seems simple. Which is why it's so difficult.

Chapter Eleven: Build an Audience from Scratch

(Stephen)

All of this content-building is fruitless without an audience that finds it valuable. Odds are, your agency has a small list of prospects, people who like your Facebook page or subscribers to the newsletter you publish every so often. But you're going to need a larger, hungrier audience for your authority positioning to serve your agency in a meaningful way. Building an audience from scratch will work for your agency even if you're just getting started creating your cornerstone content, if you need to make an audience from scratch, and if you don't have a paid media budget.

We didn't include paid media for several reasons. There are already some excellent books written on how to execute paid media campaigns, so we didn't feel the need to re-invent the wheel. In addition, if your agency is narrowly focused on several niches as we recommended in Chapters Three and Four, then buying access to a broad audience is an investment you can and should avoid.

To dominate your niches and drive biz-dev for your agency, you don't need a million downloads of your podcast episodes. You don't need 10,000 YouTube subscribers. But what you do need is an audience that is hungry to learn from you, is intrigued by your point of view, and from a biz-dev perspective, can drive revenue for your agency.

Here's the reality. If your agency is like most small to mid-sized agencies we work with, you would be hard pressed to onboard and service more than four to five new, right-sized (5 to 10 percent of your annual AGI) clients a year without needing to adjust your capacity and workflow. Most agencies aren't in the position to onboard 10, 20, or 50 new clients for 12 months.

If that sounds like your agency, fight the temptation to build a large audience for your cornerstone content just for ego or because in our world, we're so used to chasing the biggest audience we can find. In this case, it's a wasted effort and more about vanity numbers. None of which will move your agency's biz-dev forward.

Instead, we think Kevin Kelly, founder of *Wired Magazine*, was spot-on when he wrote his essay, "1,000 True Fans." The strategy is just as relevant today as when Kevin wrote it in 2008. The full text as well as the long-tail curve he created to illustrate the 1,000 true fans strategy can be found at http://kk.org/thetechnium/1000-true-fans.

To paraphrase the strategy, Kevin describes "true fans" as prospects, clients, and industry-related peers who will help you mobilize and move your agency to the next level. They are true fans of you, true fans of being students of your teachings, and true fans of the results of your agency's work. They will support you because of the connection and loyalty you've built with them through the value you share within your consistent cornerstone content. Whether you do that every day or every week, no matter what the schedule, no matter what the rhythm, the fact that you're consistently helpful is what's essential to your true fans.

Kevin defines "a true fan" as someone who will purchase anything and everything you produce. True fans will drive 200 miles to visit your office for a party. They will engage your team for the super deluxe, platinum service package when you roll it out, even if they are currently working with your agency at the standard level.

They have a Google Alert set for your and your agency's name. They've bookmarked your website. They come to your special events. They come to your book signings and ask for you to sign their copies. They cannot wait for your agency's next webinar, your next podcast episode to air, or your next event. If that sounds far-fetched, we promise you, it isn't. You can become that relevant to your audience. You can provide enough value that they're confident in whatever you might do next— you have become an absolute authority in their minds.

The best way to increase your agency's AGI is to connect with your true fans directly. All you need is cornerstone content focused on being helpful and delivering value, and your true fans will love you for it. Building an audience of 1,000 true fans over time is a reasonable goal for your agency, even if you're focused on the narrowest of niches. It might take some time and hard work, but it's possible for your agency to reach this goal through organic growth alone. Remember, an email opt-in you receive from a Facebook campaign isn't a true fan. But they can be converted into one. Now, someone who finds your content, loves your content, sees value in your content, and subscribes to it because they cannot imagine missing a single episode—yep, that's a true fan.

But how do you organically build an audience of true fans specifically aligned with the niches your agency serves? Building an audience from scratch, if you go it alone, takes a significant amount of time, and you can certainly go that route. Fortunately, you don't have to do it that way. It's much easier to take advantage of other people's networks, connections, and passion by creating content they want to share with their audience. If your audience aligns with theirs, and your content's truly helpful, they'll be excited to share it and collaborate with you.

You can go at this a couple of ways. The first is to actually include other people in the creation of your content and have them share the results. The second is to find other experts who have a media channel of their own (podcast, blog, etc.), and create content worthy of their attention.

Let's look at the co-creation aspect first. Your cornerstone content could be a blog, a video series, a podcast, a collection of articles, or perhaps a book. By interviewing people as part of the content-creation process, you're generating a very useful tool—a guest list. This will be one of your most valuable assets in building your audience from scratch.

Your guests will become your advocates, your "sneezers," by sharing your content through to their audience. Some of their listeners, email subscribers, and social media followers will also become your audience. But this can only happen if you get strategic from the beginning.

Let's start with how you organize your initial guest list. Your guests for the first 10 to 15 episodes of your podcast, or blog posts, or video series, etc., should be colleagues, people you know, whom you can be candid with, as in this proposal, for example: "Hey Sara. I'm launching a podcast serving X industry, and it would really mean a lot to me if you'd be one of my first guests. I don't know how successful the new show will be, but I know you, and we'll have a fun conversation! And our audience will love you because you'll help them think about X. Would you be willing to schedule time using my online calendar here [insert your link]?"

Sara will likely say yes to this invitation because she's a friend or a professional colleague. Interview Sara and highlight her depth of expertise around the topic you mentioned in your invitation. Air the episode, post the blog post, upload the video, etc., but also share the content with your social media audiences and email subscriber lists, no matter how small. When you share the content, stay away from self-promotion, and don't mention that it's your first episode, or celebrate the launch of the channel. Instead, just celebrate Sara, her smarts, her expertise, and how her insights around Topic X will be useful to your audience. Put her out front. Then tag Sara in all of your social media posts. All of your tweets. All of your Facebook posts. All of your LinkedIn posts. Tag her in all channels most relevant to your niches. And add Sara's email address to your distribution list so that when you share her expertise, she'll receive it in her inbox, too.

Your team can coordinate all of this activity to happen on the day Sara's episode airs or is published. Know what happens when it does? Sara's notifications and inboxes lights up. She's overwhelmed with comments, likes, and perhaps some shares. That level of excitement motivates her to share your posts with her community or possibly forward your email to her own subscriber list because it's an opportunity for her to share her own thought leadership and add value to her audience.

Again, you make the sharing more likely when you put Sara out front in the content. She is more apt to like it, comment on it, and share it with her audience. In the process of her doing that, more people become aware of you, and your channels get some social proof. This is vital early on as you're building your audience.

Your next step is to wash, rinse, and repeat the process you used with Sara for your next set of guests. When you do that, you create a sound initial foundation of social proof for your content across multiple channels. Fifteen shows or posts into the development will give you enough credibility to begin to reach out to people you don't know as well, or at all. You'll have some early stats in terms of audience.

Now's the time to begin reaching out to your nano set of top 25 prospects, those prospects that are within the niches your agency serves, and invite them to be your featured guests. It's likely they'll review some of the content you've posted on your website and social channels as part of their due diligence. But your invitation will be easy to say yes to when they see the level of engagement your posts with your first several guests have garnered.

An important distinction here is not to limit your invitations to your targeted prospect list. You want to mix it up with other subject matter experts and guests who have an audience you want to get in front of, as well.

Your criteria for *all* guests should be 1) can they teach my audience something that will help them do their job better? and 2) are they a prospect, or are they someone who has an audience of my sweet-spot prospects? To be one of your featured guests, you must always be able to say yes to number one, and most of the time, to number two, as well.

This strategy not only helps build an initial audience from scratch, but quite honestly, it will boost your confidence and keep you from getting nervous about reaching out to a more high-profile guest that might really help put you on the map. You'll see an increase in downloads and web traffic, email subscribers, and social media followers as a result of this initial work. But your key to long-term success with this strategy will be consistency. Each episode, blog post, video, or other piece of cornerstone content needs to be shared with your guests in the same way.

In Chapters Thirteen and Fifteen, we will share some systems, tips, and tricks that will help you and your team scale this effort. If you keep slicing, dicing, sharing, and posting week after week, 52 weeks a year, you will quickly outpace every other agency you typically compete against.

If you decide to produce cornerstone content that requires a different strategy than bringing on guests, you can still leverage other people to build your audience more quickly. Make a list of publications, people, podcasts, events, etc. that all target the same audience you have your efforts focused on. Earn their attention by beginning to consume, comment on, and share their content on your (your personal and the agency's) social channels. These are people you need to know, whether they are willing to return the favor or not. But when it comes to content sharing, there is an implied reciprocity that almost always occurs.

Even the most popular or famous of thought leaders and experts will welcome your attention and notice that you're expanding their reach. Associations and other organizations that serve your target audience will be even more thrilled because they rarely get that kind of support. And you can put that sharing on some sort of autopilot like dlvr.it so you keep showing up as a fan.

Now reach out and introduce yourself. Share some of your best content with them and ask them if they think their audience would find it valuable. A few will decline initially, but they will all start watching what you're creating. But most, even though you may just be starting off, will be happy to introduce your channel to their audience.

There's nothing wrong with using both methods if your content creation lends itself to both. Even if you don't do anything we've outlined in this chapter, you will build an audience if you stay true to the mantra, "Will this content help my audience be better at their job?" every time you publish a piece of content. Your authority position will be borne from that effort.

Before we close out this chapter and move on to how to turn this effort into a revenue stream, we want to take you behind the scenes on how we built the content for this chapter. Stephen originally shared many of the foundational elements of this chapter as part of his weekly video series on YouTube. You can find the short video here: https://bit.ly/2PzDN9P.

It's another example of how cornerstone content that was initially created for a YouTube series could be re-tooled a little bit and re-purposed into a book chapter, as was the case here. As we keep promising, you and your team don't need to reinvent the wheel every time to have a consistent flow of new content.

Chapter Twelve: How to Monetize Your Content

(Stephen)

Many agency owners, when thinking about creating content for their own agency or explaining away why they don't do it well or consistently, talk about the cost of the effort. One of our goals with this book is to help you realize that when you make the effort to develop your authority position in the marketplace, you turn that cost into revenue, and you can and will get paid for your efforts.

As we mentioned in an earlier chapter, there are two broad categories for the revenue you can make from a smart content strategy. The first and most obvious is direct revenue. That includes things like winning a new client (biz-dev), or someone paying you for a course, a class, your book, or some other offering. For many agencies, this is the only revenue stream they're interested in. They just want finding and winning new clients to be faster and easier. There's nothing wrong with stopping right there.

But others may be intrigued by the idea of diversifying revenue streams, and we're good with that, too. Let's look at the direct side of things first. Even if you do nothing else, your content is going to get you noticed, assuming you're consistent in both your efforts and your focus. As prospects shop around for potential agency partners, your name will show up. It might be from a Google search, an appearance at a trade show, a podcast interview they listen to, or through some other means. That alone will put you into consideration sets that you otherwise would never have been a part of.

But you can put some gasoline on that fire by using the Trojan horse of sales. As we've said before, it starts by recognizing that your nano list of 25 prospects can also be part of your content-creation strategy. By interviewing those prospects and putting the spotlight on them, you're in essence putting the light onto yourself, too. Your audience just doesn't recognize it as such.

Leveraging your cornerstone content in the form of a Trojan horse gives you the opportunity to demonstrate your smarts in a casual business conversation with one of your prospects instead of through an agency pitch. Your prospect's guard is down, they're engaged in the interview, and you have created the opportunity for them to lean into what you're sharing and to eventually ask you to tell them a little more about what your agency does.

The stage is set to begin a relationship with your nano 25 prospect, and it never felt like biz-dev at all to either of you, and that's a beautiful thing.

You're probably familiar with the legend of the Trojan horse from The Iliad, the famous tale of the war between the Greeks and the city of

Troy. The story is an excellent illustration of smart strategy that works as well today as it did back then. According to the legend, the Trojan War almost ended in a stalemate because Greece was unable to devise a strategy to circumvent the city walls of Troy. After a 10-year siege, the Greek army made what looked to be a retreat to their homeland. The Trojan army investigated and found the beach abandoned. The Greek armada was gone, and a large wooden horse was all that remained on the desolate shore. The Trojans believed the Greeks had left the horse as a peace offering. They gleefully accepted the offering and pulled the horse from the beach, past their impenetrable city gates, and into the city square, where they began to celebrate their victory.

However, a little due diligence by the Trojans would have been prudent. Perhaps they would have found the Greek strike force tucked inside the horse. The Greeks seized their opportunity late that night when they snuck quietly out of the horse and opened the city gates so the remaining balance of their army could enter. The Greeks proceeded to sack the city, and the story gave birth to the expression, "Beware a Greek bearing gifts."

There's an important distinction between what the Greeks did and what we are suggesting when it comes to using a Trojan horse. They did it to win a battle and destroy a city. It was deceptive and destructive. We're not suggesting either. We're using the analogy because in the agency world, we often talk about how hard it is to get past a prospect's gatekeeper or to get our foot in the door.

You aren't going to hide the fact that you're an agency owner. Or that you serve businesses in your potential client's sector. You aren't going to do any damage with anything they share with you. You are just knocking on a different door, wearing your publisher hat versus your biz-dev hat, a door they're more likely to open willingly and invite you into so you can begin to create a relationship. You're still going to switch hats at some point (at their invitation, of course) and sell when the time comes. But selling isn't how you make that first connection.

We can still learn from the Greeks' success. A typical agency owner or business development person often hits a brick wall when they're making sales calls or inquiries. No big shock there; we do it to vendors every day. But when you show up not as the agency's sales arm but instead as a media publisher, you're met with a different reaction. When you write a monthly column for your niche's trade publication, or you're the author of a blog featuring marketing ideas and trends in your niche industry, or your agency is conducting a primary research study focused on the niche that the prospective company operates in, you're seen through a different lens. A more hospitable lens.

Now, when you reach out to the decision-maker on your nano 25 list to say you'd like to interview him or her about their journey, their secrets to success, and the wisdom they could share with others in the industry, you're welcomed, not shooed away or ignored. You just changed the conversation to something they're interested in pursuing.

Your cornerstone content just increased the probability of a one-on-one, private, sixty-minute conversation with one of your best prospects. But how did you get that kind of all-access pass? You were able to change the game because you're no longer perceived as an agency owner looking for a new client. You're now seen as a *journalist*, and your column, YouTube series, blog, podcast, or whatever cornerstone content channel you selected, becomes a conduit to an audience the guests you interview wants to reach and influence. All of a sudden, you've become the gatekeeper! The roles are completely reversed; now your potential client is knocking on your door and asking for access to your audience.

You now have an opportunity to dazzle your prospect with your smarts during the interview and post-interview conversations, without ever having to sell. The key to this strategy is to keep being helpful to that guest, long after the initial conversation or interview. As we've said before, in the nano level of the sales funnel, you're going to nurture this new relationship with incredible generosity and in helping this prospect get better at their job.

Because you've already formed a relationship with them, they're going to be open to hearing from you and will find even more value in whatever you send to them. At some point (and remember, it could take a day or a decade), they will either hire you, refer business to you, or open some doors for you. In any case, you will monetize that relationship.

But you don't have to create content via the guest model. And you don't have to sell to your guests, if you have them. It's just a way of accelerating the most direct ROI—new clients for your agency.

The indirect ROI of the authority marketing strategy is that you build a loyal audience (ala Kevin Kelly's "1,000 True Fans") and then you can either sell to them directly or you can sell access to them via sponsorships and other offerings. That's part of what we call "the Trident of Monetization."

The Trident of Monetization

Let's keep rolling with the Greek mythology references by introducing you to the Trident of Monetization! As the name implies, there are three parts, or prongs, to this strategy, the indirect monetization model. Remember, this is optional and in addition to direct monetization. We're not suggesting that anyone would build an authority position to take advantage of the indirect sales opportunities.

But why not ask yourself the question, "Now that we're actively using this content strategy to woo and win clients, how else can it serve me as the owner, or the entire agency?"

With the trident, you truly need to begin thinking of your agency as a media company, and each category of cornerstone content now represents a media property you can leverage and monetize. For example, your podcast, your email, your social media communities, your YouTube channel, and even your blog, are all media properties. That research project you've considered doing? You guessed it—it's a media property, too. Each content channel you create is likely a media property. And that means you have a lot to sell to a third-party brand once you build enough of an audience for each property.

Let's review the three prongs of the trident to illustrate how content and audience are at the center of this strategy. To be clear, you don't need a large audience to be successful with the trident. You just need an active, engaged, and narrowly defined audience. This matters when it comes time to approach a third-party brand to sell a sponsorship, or if you plan to sell products or services directly to that audience, other than traditional agency services.

Prong 1: Build an active audience around your authority position. One easy way to do this is to still co-create content with guests, but the guests are not potential clients for your agency. In this scenario, they're experts who can also be helpful to your prospects and in fact would be eager to be on your show because you share the same prospect profile. Your audience is their audience.

Ideally, these are other thought leaders who complement your areas of expertise and also have audiences of their own. Give serious consideration to how each guest will deliver value to your audience. What examples can they share, what can they teach, what big idea can they inspire with your audience? There's an important balance here. You definitely want to surround yourself with super-smart and generous professionals who can help you attract an audience and provide valuable content, but you don't want to only be the conduit to other experts. You need to establish your own expertise, too. You absolutely can do that through your interactions with the guest expert, but you'll also want to balance your co-creation pieces with content you create on your own so your own depth of expertise can shine through.

If you don't want to involve other people, that's a fine choice, as well. You just need to create killer content on your own. In either option, the point here is to create a first prong that builds an audience in all the ways we've talked about in previous chapters. Naturally, it will be faster if you have guests, and they share your content with their audience. But in any case, you don't need an enormous audience. Narrowly defined wins over volume every time.

These indirect methods of making money off your content are definitely a long-term play. It's highly likely you will need at least 12 months of creating cornerstone content, sharing content, asking for reviews, building your email list, and other success metrics before you're ready to move on.

Prong 2: Sell access to your audience. We're not talking nickels and pennies flowing into your agency with this prong of the trident. We're talking about $10,000 to $100,000 in one payday. Without doing any additional work! That's a pretty good day for most small to mid-sized agencies. And now someone's paying you to do biz-dev and create content. Not a bad gig.

Prong 2 typically takes the form of ad sales, or a sponsorship across one or several of your properties. You are media company now. You get to decide pricing, what to include in the packages you choose to offer, the level of access a sponsor can have with your audience, and the duration of the deal. All the details need to be presented in a professional, industry-standard sponsor proposal.

The full sponsor proposal is about eight to 10 pages in length and typically includes:

- A description of each property you are making available for ad placement or sponsorship, including frequency of content creation, the creators involved, how long you've been publishing, the size of the audience, etc. Again, your podcast is a property. Your website is a property, and so on. Wherever people obtain your content is a media property.

- Your sponsor's goals. Perhaps they're interested in increasing brand loyalty or their customer base, or educating people, or driving traffic, leads, or sales. But you need to acknowledge their goals just like you would during a new business presentation with a prospective client.

- A one-page marketing plan. It contains all the ways the buyer is going to get exposure. For ad placements, this is pretty simple, but for sponsorships, you need to include more details. Sponsors are interested in being associated with your content because it attracts an audience they care about, and they derive value from association with your brand. Outline the ways they get that exposure.

- Your demographics. Whether your demographics are mothers, the parent market, the entrepreneurial market, urban youth, or baby boomers, you need to describe them. Include any testimonials or feedback you have collected.

- The ad placement or sponsorship fees for each property. We are currently seeing podcasts get sponsored for anywhere from $12,000 to as much as $30,000 annually. That fee increases to upwards of $40,000 annually when the host was able to include the sponsor in live events as well. We've also seen a single eBook get sponsored for $12,000 and small events sponsored for $3,500 to $5,000. The bottom line is that the pricing strategy will be driven by your relationship with the prospective sponsor and have less to do with standardized industry pricing because at this stage, there is no such thing. The harder your audience is to reach, the more valuable the opportunity is to potential partners.

- Your story. Help them understand your community, your commitment to that community, and the connections and relationships you've built. Make it a very human connection. As a creative and strategic agency, you will likely have a significant advantage over others competing for sponsorship dollars because you tell stories every day.

We also want to share some words on typical questions sponsors may ask you during the various stages of the negotiation. There are no right or wrong answers. But always protect your audience when deciding how to respond. If your audience feels like you're using them, and that eclipses the value you bring them, they'll bolt. And without an audience, none of this is possible.

A sponsor may ask you:

- How many guests can they can place onto media property, if you have guests? Will you be comfortable with that?
- Will you provide an exclusive sponsorship meaning no representatives from competing companies as guests on your show or no other sponsors at all? If so, is there an additional cost for the exclusivity?
- Will you give them influence or control over your content? (We'd

suggest that should be a deal-breaker for you. You need to protect your audience and the editorial integrity of what you're creating because ultimately, it's your intellectual property, so you want to be sure you have control over it.)

• Will you share your email list with them? As you know, there are all kinds of implications and complications with this request. So be ready for it.

Prong 3: Sell to your audience. As you move through the first two prongs, you will be presented (or encouraged to provide your listeners) with opportunities to do business with you. Some in your audience may ask you to host an event or create a mastermind group or inner-circle offering where they get face time with you or your team. Some may ask you to package up your thought leadership to sell it as a course. A literary agent may reach out to you because she's been listening to your podcast or just heard you speak at a conference last weekend and would like to represent you on a book deal. You might create workshop or coaching content and offer that to your audience. As you create more content and get to know your audience better, the options will begin to appear, as you think about how you can genuinely add more value for them.

Many of you help your clients build out their value ladder. How do they go from getting a non-customer to make that first small purchase to turning that fledgling customer into a recurring one?

There's no reason why you can't do the same thing with the audience you've earned through your authority position. Your content is the first (and the free) rung of the ladder. What would your audience value next? How do you take them from that free consumption to a reasonably risk-free purchase, like buying a book? From there, it's up to you (and what your prospects need) to build out a value ladder of offerings that allow them to get more of your smarts in whatever way they value most.

As agency owners and leaders, we rarely think this way. We sell agency services, that's what we do. But is that all we can do?

Imagine what multiple revenue streams would do for your cash flow and for balancing out the ebbs and flows that are native to agency life. You should consider and tuck away all those pre-conceived notions about what an agency sells and think about your agency's value ladder in a new light. For example, you could:

- host a paid industry event for your niches.
- host high-ticket mastermind groups.
- charge for introduction or vendor meet-ups.
- sell access to an inner-circle membership.
- book speaking engagements.
- sell courses.
- publish books.
- publish research.
- And that's just scratching the surface!

Your ability to produce cornerstone content is what gives you and your agency the opportunities to create a robust value ladder. And when you look at the above list, you don't see any agency services, do you? All of the revenue flowing into your agency from your value ladder is the result of your content creation and the position of authority it creates for you. Yes, it will require work, but it's all possible and will go a long way in sustaining and growing your agency.

Chapter Thirteen: Yes, You Can Get it All Done!

(Stephen)

At this point, we're going to assume you see the value in creating an authority position. But you might still be thinking, "This would be amazing, and it sounds effective, but I don't have the time. Or talent. Or whatever."

We know how crazy your days are. How you run from fire to fire and don't get to actually dent your to-do list until late in the day or after the kids crash for the night. So how are you going to write a book? Or record a podcast every week or write articles?

We are so glad you asked. This chapter and the appendix section marked "Tools" will help. We're not going to lie to you; we have no access to magic wands. It'll definitely take work to make it happen. But this work is very doable, especially if you now see the ROI of making the effort.

No matter what channel you choose, it's going to require you to exercise some muscles that might have atrophied a little. You're going to have to reignite the journalist, the teacher, the writer, and the student in you. Most agency owners love this new focus once they get started. It's the perfect combination of getting smarter at every turn and helping others do the same.

It's also going to require your team to pitch in. That may be to take other work off your plate to free up your time, but in most cases, creating an authority position becomes an agency-wide project. We may never hear their voices or see their faces, but they're your production crew, your ideation team, your project managers, and your marketing department. It would be almost impossible to do this on your own.

But most of all, it's going to take discipline on your part.

Every channel is not created equal. Writing a book is a much bigger task than partnering with a research firm and paying them to conduct primary research. Hosting an interview-style podcast is much less time-consuming than writing a weekly in-depth blog post. As you begin to decide which channel is right for you, how much time it's going to take has to be a factor.

Your calendar isn't going to make this easy. At least not today. We've never met an agency owner who had a lot of free time on their hands. But you can start blocking an hour or two a week out of your calendar to dedicate to this work, and if you go out a few weeks, maybe a half a day every week.

You can develop and deliver high quality content via any of the channels we've discussed, if you can protect three to five hours a week. Is more time than that ideal? Of course, but it's not necessary.

In three to five hours a week, you can:

- write half a chapter for your book.
- record at least four podcast episodes.
- write an article for a trade pub.
- write three blog posts.
- record 10 three-minute videos.
- review one phase of a research project.

You get the idea. Don't let the time excuse win. For most agency owners, once they get started, they actually enjoy the creation, and suddenly, it's easier to get on the calendar.

We're guessing you're already an over-achiever and get more done in a week than most people do in a month. That's how entrepreneurs roll. If you find yourself offering up the time excuse, look to see what's underneath that protestation. If you're like most people, it's fear.

There are several hacks for multiplying your efforts. See if any of these help you see a new path to diving into content creation.

One Plus One Makes Three?

You may be able to take content from a current cornerstone channel and, without too much effort, twist it into another stand-alone piece. This book is a perfect example.

From time to time, the two of us will team up and co-teach a workshop for the AMI audience. As we were preparing the content for a 2018 workshop, we realized that the depth of content we had prepared could form a solid foundation for a book—this book.

As we taught the workshop, we recorded the audio of the entire two-day workshop with the consent of all attendees. We then used the transcripts to build out the chapters you're reading now. We estimate it cut our writing time in half at the very minimum. It also gave us a chance to test out some of the messaging to see what resonated with agency owners.

If you give a lot of presentations, teach internal lunch-and-learns, or offer webinars, these are all excellent kindling for a book or a series of keynote speeches or an article series. Look for ways that one cornerstone channel can help you create a one-time spin-off.

Can You Go Backwards?

What about going the opposite direction? Could you generate smaller pieces of content you could build into a book? Many agency owners have outlined something big, typically a book or video series, then divided up that outline into micro-elements or topics. From there, they took each micro section and wrote a stand-alone blog post for each one. After they amassed a year's worth of these smaller elements, they knitted them together into a book or other cornerstone channel, like a video series or podcast.

Let Someone Else Do the Heavy Lifting

We've talked several times about the perks of interviewing other people and leveraging their smarts to augment your own. Some of those experts might be closer than you think!

When I was writing my book, *Profitable Podcasting*, I sat down and interviewed members of my team to document their technical expertise for the middle chapters of the book. The technical magic didn't come from me, it came from the Predictive ROI (PROI) team, and they're cited as the source within the book, which is a fun, brag-worthy thing for your employees, by the way.

As *Profitable Podcasting* was nearing completion, my agent passed on a curveball thrown by the publisher. They requested that a chapter on sponsorships be included in the book. Back then, PROI didn't have a depth of expertise in sponsorships, so how could I write a chapter on the topic? My agent was able to connect me to an expert in securing sponsorships that I interviewed for Chapter Sixteen of the book. The interview was also aired as Episode 383 of Onward Nation, creating slicing and dicing opportunities off the cornerstone of the episode.

Another way to get other people involved in helping you make this happen is by hiring them to do some of the work. Whether it's for a book, an article series, or some other written content you're going to shape into your authority position's hub, you could hire a ghostwriter. This adds another layer of production cost, but it can make your efforts super-efficient. The ghostwriter can interview you, tap into your depth of knowledge, and then craft the channel's content from there, capturing your personal style and tone, as well.

If you're choosing primary research as your cornerstone channel, you almost always have to let someone else do the lion's share of the work, unless that's your background. For research to work as a differentiator, it has to be beyond reproach. People are going to question the data if you can't demonstrate that the research itself was conducted properly.

You and your team will determine the focus of the research, weigh in on the questions, and maybe they will help you write and design the final version of the report and data visualization. But unless you have a research expert on staff, your research partner is going to do the heavy bulk of the data collection and statistical analysis.

Leverage the Tools, the People, and Processes You Already Have

If anyone should be able to pull of this content strategy, it's us. We have everything we need at our fingertips because we already do this on a regular basis for our clients. Use that to your advantage.

Create a client code for your work positioning yourself as an authority. Open jobs, traffic them, and assign tasks to your team (and to yourself). Assign them to your best, most persistent account executive, and ask them to herd you and your entire team.

Play to your strengths. Your entire career has been deadline-driven, and most of us are hardwired not to miss one. I'm pretty sure neither of us would be nearly as prolific if we hadn't assigned deadlines for our content (these being simply an internal deadline based on the audience's expectation of new content, regularly posted), and if we weren't being nagged by our production teams.

Last, but by no means least, make a commitment. Make it to yourself, and make it publicly to your team. Help them see why this matters and how it can change the trajectory of your agency. Then honor that commitment to show them just how vital you believe it to be.

Any of these smart shortcuts are viable options for you. But at a certain point, this is either important to you, or it isn't. We're never too busy for the things we deeply want to do or know we must do. We believe this is a must-do. If you share that belief, you'll find a way.

But wait, there's more. Creating the cornerstone content isn't enough on its own. You have to maximize that effort by turning that cornerstone into many cobblestones.

Slicing and Dicing Your Cornerstone Content

Earlier in the book, we asked you to consider the question, "Would you prefer to talk or write?" Then we encouraged you to choose a cornerstone channel for your content that would allow you to easily build cobblestones from that core.

Now it's time to learn how to slice and dice your cornerstone content into those cobblestones we keep talking about. The section of the appendix called "The Slice and Dice Recipes" will give you and your team a framework for taking one piece of cornerstone content and transforming it into 50, 100, 150-plus additional pieces of content.

Why is this element of our strategy so important? Here's the reality, whether you believe it or not: Once you get started, it's reasonably easy to get into the discipline of producing a single piece of content on a regular basis. But if you want to accelerate and build your reputation as a true authority, it boils down to findability. Having cobblestones out there, acting as beacons and shining a light back to the hub of your content, makes all the difference in the world. Each piece is a multiplier, increasing the odds that your next new client will stumble upon your agency and begin to soak up your smarts.

Don't minimize your efforts. Be sure your team creates a repeatable system to make sure that everything you create is immediately converted into 10 or more pieces of useful content that you can use and re-use.

In the next chapter, you're going to meet some of the agencies who have brought everything we've been writing about to life. Notice how much of their success is tied to their agency's ability to re-purpose, re-package, and re-use every bit of value that comes from their cornerstone channel.

Chapter Fourteen:
Agencies Doing it Well

(Drew)

I'm guessing that throughout the book there's been this nagging little voice in the back of your head that keeps telling you that all of this is nice in theory, but that no agency can actually make it happen for themselves. You've probably offered yourself the oft-uttered "cobbler's children have no shoes" excuse more than once.

You don't have to take our word for it. Agencies are doing exactly what we're describing in this book, and it is paying huge dividends. Let me introduce you to some agencies and share with you their authority position strategies and efforts and the wins that are a direct result.

Industrial

Industrial is a brand and growth strategy agency that specializes in the industrial B2B niche, helping their clients do everything from recruiting employees to taking new products to market. It even says so in their name!

Industrial is located in Nashville and has 30 employees. Their authority position is clearly their niche—the B2B industrial section. Agency owner James Soto is driving much of the content creation, and the effort started in January of 2018. They have two cornerstone channels. One is the stand-alone website Industrial Marketer (IndustrialMarketer.com), which earns the agency 30,000 unique visitors a month.

The other is their YouTube channel, *Industrial Strength Marketing*, where they launch and house informational videos. They push each new video out on LinkedIn, as well. Typically, they'll get about 7,000 views on that channel alone. This is important to consider, as one video repurposed natively for LinkedIn can outperform months of videos in the early stages of building a niche on YouTube.

They also atomize content for Facebook and Instagram. All of that drives traffic to James's speaking page, jamessoto.com, and their agency website.

Every channel they manage is integrated in some way. They make it a point to slice and dice their content to maximize distribution, discoverability, and conversion. Cross-promotion on IndustrialMarketer.com with native ads feeds lead-generation for the agency, as well.

One of the biggest wins that Industrial points to is that their clients notice and mention their videos and the value they offer. They've also received business opportunities from prospects because of their video series, including a billion-dollar industrial company in Tennessee. The video series and the stand-alone website have opened up more speaking opportunities and podcast interviews than the agency has ever had before.

Avocet

Avocet is located in Colorado, with offices in Longmont and Denver. Their niches are asset-intensive technology brands, entrepreneurial start-ups, and expanding small to midsize retail businesses. Their unique POV is tied to how they build out full-funnel strategies with some very innovative technologies and insights.

Their cornerstone channel is the *Integrate and Ignite* podcast, which they've been producing since 2017 with agency owner Lori Jones hosting the show. They've sliced and diced that weekly content and the exposure it affords them into category-specific microsites they can mention during the show and in social media content, blogs, visuals like quote cards, videos, e-books, email, and during many speaking engagements.

Lori often gets invited by industry-leading tradeshows like the International Association of Chiefs of Police (IACP) and NetSuite to be their guest at the show, to interview their keynote speakers, and to serve as a guest influencer.

The team at Avocet is very metrics-driven, so they've been measuring the ROI of the effort from the beginning. Today, they enjoy six times their ROI on new business they've won through the show, and their Google visits have increased more than 700 percent since airing their first episode.

Crema

Crema is a product design studio located in Kansas City, Mo. Their authority position is that they can help clients bring a software idea to life. They work alongside their clients to ideate, build a minimally viable prototype, beta test that prototype, and take the software to market.

The lion's share of their work is with product owners and managers of B2B software solutions within enterprise organizations, as well as experienced technical founders of rapid-growth startups. Their area of expertise is in the user experience layer of a web or mobile application in collaboration with a data or API partner inside or outside the client's current team.

Their cornerstone channel is YouTube, though it's all aggregated and managed back to the Crema.us website through dedicated landing pages or blog posts so they can track conversions. The YouTube channel allows them to share their culture, their thought leadership, and their ability to stay relevant on the newest strategies, tools, and tactics in the digital product industry.

They do a masterful job of slicing and dicing their content across multiple platforms.

Podcast: This has been the primary platform for the co-owners, George Brooks and Dan X, to speak to the tactics of creating and growing an effective product culture, mixed with interviews from the team as well as other thought leaders in the industry. It's led to many introductions to people reaching out to learn more.

Hype Videos: These short native videos for LinkedIn and Instagram are a great way to go back into their video archives and repurpose old content into something new.

Native Videos: While YouTube is their fastest-growing channel, they find that posting a tailored video natively to Facebook, LinkedIn, and Instagram performs better for their algorithms.

Medium.com Articles: This is a hot topic, but they post to both their blog and their Medium channel, using the Medium importer so that it doesn't down-rank them in terms of SEO. The medium infrastructure for promoting content around topics is very powerful. They know that their product management audience is very active on the platform, so it's a smart place for them to be.

Blog Posts: SEO is still a very powerful tool, and in 2019, writing to take advantage of it has urged them to step up their game and become much more intentional with headlines and content, and the results are paying off as they watch people navigate from a blog post to other pages of their sites and forms of content.

Their authority position work has scored some huge wins for them. A client in early 2019 was generated directly from a development team watching their video on React vs. Flutter. The prospect told their leadership that Crema was exactly the agency they'd prefer to collaborate with, and it was one of the fastest sales cycles in Crema's history.

Given that their contract sizes are often in the six figures, their clients are often doing their due diligence to learn more about the company they're considering partnering with. Crema rarely responds to RFPs, so clients need to have a way to build early trust with the Crema team. Nearly all of Crema's clients mention that they've spent time on their YouTube channel or listening to their podcasts which re-affirmed their excitement to work with a company with a culture like theirs.

But the wins aren't just about biz-dev for Crema. Their Instagram and YouTube channels are incredible recruiting tools. They're in a very in-demand industry for talent acquisition. While most other companies and agencies have utilized recruiters, the Crema team finds that a lot of their recruitment traffic can be tracked through links from their Instagram and YouTube channels, and nearly all their applicants—

which are many, even without dedicated recruitment strategies—mention they have watched Crema's videos and are willing to do anything to work for a company like theirs. Dan and George credit their authority-positioned marketing for their amazing pipeline of talent, and in a time when most agencies are struggling to find a worthy candidate, Crema has the cream of the crop to choose from, which has allowed them to grow from 20 to 43 employees!

Gumas

Gumas is a full-service branding, advertising, and digital marketing agency located in San Francisco. They have 10 full-time equivalent (FTE) employees and augment their staff with specialists as needed. Their authority position is that they are the champions of the Challenger brand and have been actively developing and owning that position for over a decade. They've even gone as far as securing the trademark for the phrase "Challenger Brand Marketing®."

Agency owner John Gumas and his agency's president Craig Alexander are the authors of *Challenger Brand Marketing®*, and the way they wrote the book was through a carefully orchestrated schedule of blog posts. Each blog post stood on its own in terms of content, but they were also the building blocks for the book. They used the book as a new business tool, a 3-D business card of sorts, and they slice and dice that content throughout their social media channels, on their website, and in new business pitches.

They also choose a narrowly focused theme for the month, always tied to Challenger Brand Marketing®, and create additional content for their blog, which they push out through a variety of channels.

Gumas is routinely invited to pitch businesses, or awarded business outright, because of their authority position. Prospects will say, "We are totally a challenger brand, so we need a specialist like you."

Twist Image

In 2002 Mitch Joel joined a small digital agency called Twist Image in Montreal as a partner and president. Mitch was charged with growing the agency and the traditional methods of agency sales felt disingenuous to him. He decided to harness his inner journalist/publisher mindset and began producing a blog on the Twist Image site. He blogged seven days a week and his content was always focused on teaching, exploring, and innovating around the intersection of brands, consumers, and technology.

As the blog began to build an audience, podcasting was just coming into play and Mitch decided to extend his blog's reach with a weekly podcast, called Six Pixels of Separation. (It currently has about 700 episodes.) He recorded an episode every Sunday and initially thought of it as a fun way to experiment with audio. The blog/podcast combination started creating opportunities and unearthing new pathways. Mitch started to receive invitations to speak at conferences and other events and at one of his first presentations, he met a booking agent from a speaker's bureau. That led to a long strategic alliance and many more keynotes delivered all over the world.

By using the podcast to connect with other influencers, Mitch expanded his reach, sphere of influence, and connections. One of those connections made an introduction to a literary agent and voila, Mitch's first book deal was struck.

As all of the content matured, the blog remained the agency's bedrock. The podcast, speaking gigs, and books supported the effort and good things began to happen. The right prospects started knocking on the agency's door as did the right prospective team members. Mitch was invited to serve as Chairman of the Board for the Canadian Marketing Association, influencing the industry that had served him well. Even the board meeting for the Association served as a platform for Twist Image's view of the world and led to biz-dev conversations they might not have otherwise had.

Of course, all of this activity came with a price tag. Twist Image invested heavily in making Mitch's time available for content creation and dissemination. It treated the agency as an important client and allocated budget to support the effort.

Mitch would be the first to tell you that, in some ways, it was easier back then. There wasn't as much noise and he and his team were able to carve out their own place within the relative quiet. But they also did it without the many tools, wide-spread adoption for blogs and podcasts, and distribution channels that you have available to you today. Looking back, it sounds like it was all some sort of grand plan. But everyone at the agency didn't truly see the potential of this effort right off the bat. Mitch created all of the content on his own time in the early days, trying to create a proof of concept.

"It was never about having my face on the cover of a magazine. It was about publishing content that would help the reader or listener be better at their job," Mitch explained. "You have to build your authority position on a content strategy that lives in service of your audience, not just to get some attention."

Everything was going well. They'd opened a Toronto office and were looking to expand even more. There was some conversation about buying another small agency and then they started some exploratory conversations with WPP. Eventually WPP purchased Twist Image and they became part of a worldwide conglomerate of agencies. In the documentation that outlined the value the small Canadian agency would bring to the global powerhouse, there were five key reasons that they were of value and ultimately were purchased. The first few are exactly what you'd expect – profit margins, growth, and client stability. But, one of the key reasons WPP had interest in Twist Image was because they had a platform. It became a defining point of value.

A key to the deal was that Twist Image could continue to run independently that ownership of their cornerstone content would remain theirs. A year later, WPP combined eleven digital agencies into an agency network so all eleven of the agencies, including Twist Image, became Mirum, and Mitch was named President of the Canadian division.

The podcast, speaking engagements, and blog continued to drive biz-dev for the 3,000-person agency, just like they did for the small agency start-up back in the early 2000s.

In 2018, Mitch had completed his earn out and was ready to tackle a new adventure. He was able to negotiate ownership of all of the content, book deals, and relationships he'd built over the almost 20 years as part of his departure. That serves as a good reminder to be smart about whom you allow to build your authority position. With every transition, the authority made the move, because Mitch made the move. As an owner, his efforts and notoriety became the agency's efforts and notoriety. Don't create that sort of value on rented land. Employees come and go. Make sure your authority position doesn't walk out the door with them.

This is a tale of both short and long-term gains that come from defining your niche, creating cornerstone content, and not being a one-trick pony. In the short term, the content efforts generated sales, fruitful alliances, and a leadership position in the industry. Taking the longer view, they were a key factor in agency growth, biz-dev, valuation, and ultimately acquisition.

Predictive ROI—Stephen's Agency

As you might imagine, my co-author's agency follows the authority marketing model we are teaching in this book. They have three legs on their niche stool, but all of them are built on the POV that businesses are doing sales wrong. The authority model is much faster, more effective, and more cost-efficient.

The first leg is helping agencies serve their clients. The second is helpful business owners who have built a successful company and now want to share their lessons through writing a book, consulting, or speaking, and the third is real estate investors who want to share their expertise, build audiences, and monetize their content.

Predictive's cornerstone channel is their podcast, Onward Nation. As of the summer of 2019, they are approaching episode #1,000, which is quite a feat. As you might imagine, that's a lot of remarkable content that makes slicing and dicing easy. Every episode is fragmented into social media posts and weekly email content.

One of their most effective cobblestones are the e-books they create, featuring guests who are also prospects for the agency. That serves multiple purposes. It's helpful content for their community, but it also adds value to the relationship they're building with those prospects.

In addition, they've built a resource library, they have a consistent email program, and they've built a helpful tip/idea video series that publishes a new video every week.

Their entire biz-dev strategy revolves around their content. Ninety percent of their current clients were guests on Onward Nation and experienced their comprehensive "ROI of Thought Leadership" system from a guest perspective. During their business development process, Predictive uses their own experience to basically demonstrate how the prospect could do a role reversal and be the host driving their own company's biz-dev efforts.

As the host of a top-rated podcast, Stephen receives frequent invitations to be a guest on other shows, write for publications like Forbes and Inc., and speak at events.

Echo Delta

CNP (Clark/Nikdell/Powell) is a 26-person agency located in Lakeland, Fla. They're almost 30 years old, and for many of those years, were a very high-quality generalist. They had several large anchor clients across multiple industries.

In the beginning of 2018, agency owners Alex Nikdel and Jarret Smith decided it was time to niche down. After doing their due diligence and looking at where they'd already enjoyed significant success for clients, they landed on building out their authority position as an expert in higher ed enrollment marketing for small, private colleges.

They created an agency sub-brand (Echo Delta) for this effort and began producing podcast episodes (their cornerstone channel) and augmenting them with blog posts in early 2019. They've also bought and built lists of high-value prospects, and they push their content out to that list as part of an educational series.

They consistently turn out a podcast every three weeks and a subscriber email about twice a month. That's a slower tempo than they'd like—ideally, they'd prefer to publish a podcast every other week and an email every week—but they've seen a lot of value in just being consistent and disciplined with their current schedule. This is an important reminder. Get started. Do what you can. But be consistent in the delivery, even if it's not as often as you think it should be.

Echo Delta publishes their podcast information to their blog and social media accounts, as well, slicing and dicing offerings like episode highlights in a blog post, quote graphics on social media, etc.

As a result of their efforts (keep in mind, they started producing content in 2018), Echo Delta was invited to a pitch for a small, private college half the country away from their home base. They were just awarded that business, and it's the single largest account in the agency's history!

Beyond that big win, they've generated a number of good-quality inbound leads and some great interactions with people in their target market, as well as some smaller (but still significant) wins.

Why did this happen so quickly for them? Admittedly, it's a bit of a crap shoot. It will work, but for some, it's faster than others. However, Echo Delta works incredibly hard to produce a high-quality podcast that's laser-focused on the topics their target market, higher ed enrollment and marketing leaders, care about. They stay very focused on answering the question, "How can I help our prospects be better at their job today?" Other than the closing message on the podcast, they don't ever promote the agency directly.

Don't underestimate your audience. If the content is good enough, they'll be curious about who produced it. If you deliver that consistently over time, they'll be more likely to think of you when the need for services like yours arises.

Hollywood Branded

We saved this agency for last because they're embracing this authority positioning strategy and putting it on steroids! We aren't suggesting you try to emulate what agency owner Stacy Jones has accomplished, but we are saying you can learn a lot just by watching her work.

Hollywood Branded is, as you might guess, located in Los Angeles and connects brands (directly and through partner agencies) to pop culture by leveraging partnerships through TV, film, music, events, celebrities, and influencers to create partnerships that deliver high consumer engagement. That's their niche—they deliver unique exposure through product placement and brand integration, celebrity endorsements, event sponsorships, and influencer partnerships.

The core to all of the agency's content is their blog, which receives over 25,000 unique monthly visitors. The blog started back in 2012 and didn't really take off in terms of exposure or SEO, until they combined it with emails.

Stacy and her team of nine have written a series of what they call "How To Do What Hollywood Branded Does" blog posts, with incredibly specific details about the exact steps needed to find success. Talk about answering the question, "How can I help my prospect be better at their job today?" Then they combined those posts with short teaser emails. As of 2019, they have earned 27,000 readers who receive an email once every two weeks. The email sequence is made up of more than 30 different email teasers tied back to these how-to blog posts. They get recycled over and over again. They continue to create regular blog content with a rigorous schedule of three to four new posts every week. That consistency and frequency is what makes the blog a viable cornerstone channel.

From their cornerstone, Hollywood Branded is able to slice and dice the blog posts into gated e-books, quotes, graphics, and infographics for social media channels, and because their blog posts are so meaty, easily averaging over 1,000 words, they're also producing teaser videos to drive traffic to the posts. Many of the posts are also converted into SlideShare files on LinkedIn.

They then took the how-to blog posts and knitted them together to produce two high-end reference training books, a training seminar series, and online courses (the only content they charge for). And springing from all of this written content is their agency podcast *Marketing Mistakes (And How to Avoid Them)*. Using the written content, Stacy was able to record 100 solocasts to kick off the podcast and share her methods on interviewing guests (really carefully chosen potential clients) as a biz-dev strategy.

Why would they give away all of their smarts? To quote Stacy's own words, "I'm not afraid of having our prospects, or even our clients, do the work themselves. The reality is that most won't be able to craft the same level of programs we create because they just don't have the experience. Our teaching demonstrates our value, experience, and depth of expertise over and over again. The path to closing the sale has shortened dramatically."

Why make this kind of effort? (And again, we aren't suggesting you have to do all of this to get amazing results.) Here are the wins that Hollywood Branded has enjoyed:

- Well over $1 million worth of new business.

- Invitations to pitch companies of all sizes, including those listed on the Fortune 500.

- Smart, helpful content to share with prospective clients as part of their sales process.

- A book deal in the works.

- The freedom from having to explain what their agency does on a new business sales call beyond a quick 60-second overview.

- The ability to more easily upsell current clients, as they read and watch their content and ask about other opportunities they could be leveraging.

- Opportunities for speaking engagements where Stacy can easily pull together the perfect presentation from all of the classroom materials they've created.

- Press. So much press. When reporters are looking for answers to their questions, Hollywood Branded comes up in top searches. Search for Hollywood Branded and *Game of Thrones* if you want proof.

There you have it—seven examples of agencies ranging in size from as small as eight people to as large at 46, all changing the rules of the game by attracting their sweet-spot clients to call them and ask to be a client. There's absolutely no reason why you and your agency can't enjoy that same success.

We're not saying it's easy, or that you'll see instant results, but it works. AMI is living proof. Predictive ROI is living proof. These AMI agencies are living proof.

You already have the expertise to own an authority position. Aren't you ready to put that expertise to work so you can reap the benefits?

Chapter Fifteen: The Big Close

(Drew)

If you've stuck with us this long, hopefully we've intrigued you with this idea of establishing an authority position and using it to attract prospective clients and employees like bees to a flowerbed. If there's an industry built to take advantage of this idea of authority-based marketing, it is ours. We have the skills. We have the tools. We have the people.

There are a million excuses, but it's just too competitive out there for you to be complacent. If you have a gorilla client who gives you the "luxury" of not having to chase new business, you're in the riskiest position of all. With one phone call, you can be brought to your knees, and if you don't have a sales funnel, you and your entire team could all be out looking for a job.

Here's the bottom line for all of us. We have to keep attracting, earning, and keeping new clients. It's the only way we can survive, let alone thrive. We are fighting for our lives out there. Everyone with a laptop is calling themselves an agency. Clients have a seeming infinitude of options out there, and they aren't shy about exploring them, including taking the work in-house.

If you've ever listened to my podcast, attended one of my workshops, or interacted with me, you know I believe that biz-dev is every agency owner's primary responsibility. Even if you're still in the weeds of client work, I know it weighs on you that you aren't doing more to make sure you have prospects somewhere in the sales funnel. I have never met an agency owner who isn't always thinking about, worrying about, or actively doing something to stir up some new clients.

You have four choices:

1. Wait to see what walks in the door, and take whatever you get through referrals and word-of-mouth.

2. Hope that you somehow get on a prospect's radar screen, and then compete on price in a sea of sameness with every other agency that happens to be in the mix.

3. Do the typical agency "feast or famine" biz-dev effort where you do some outbound to a large list until you win one or two clients, but your efforts die down until you're at risk of losing (or do lose) a big client, then repeat the pattern.

4. Let your content, expertise, and authority position allow you to talk to a small group of highly targeted prospects who feel like they already know, like, and trust you.

You're going to invest time, money, and effort into all of these options, even the passive waiting for referrals. You still have to meet with, pitch, woo, and win your prospects. But when you own an authority position, you do much of that work up-front and only once, as opposed to every single time there's an opportunity. By being genuinely useful and helping your prospects get better at their job every day, you're earning their faith and confidence long before you know they're out there.

By adding the nano-level and existing layers to your sales funnel, you're doing both the pull and push sides of sales. You're letting your best prospects find you toward the top of the funnel, but you're also pinpoint-targeting those 25 potential clients you know are your best bet for a successful and profitable long-term partnership. You're also enhancing your existing client relationships and reinforcing that buying decision over and over again as you grow your AGI with them.

Hopefully, after reading this book and walking through the exercises, you see the right path for your agency. You know which niches you can confidently claim and defend as your territory. You've figured out how to articulate your unique point of view that talks about how you would approach your work, and you've identified which of the many options makes the most sense in terms of choosing a cornerstone channel.

Now, like most things in life, it boils down to the decision to actually do it and making the commitment to seeing it through even when your agency is slammed, when you're about to go on vacation, and when it doesn't yield instant results.

We can't promise that you'll land your largest client within 18 months of starting the effort like Echo Delta did. But we can promise that if you do this consistently and well, it will change the future for you and your agency in some remarkable, profitable ways.

We know you can do it, absolutely. We watch, coach, and cheer on agency owners doing it every day. They're as busy as you are. They hate writing or speaking as much as you do. But they have something to say. An expertise to share with the world that their ideal prospect is hungry to get access to and learn from. And so do you. Don't waste it. Use your gifts to attract your best clients and your best profitability.

Here's the question we want to leave you with. It's only going to get more competitive out there. If you don't leverage the expertise and experience you've worked so hard to earn, how are you going to compete?

Appendix A:
Slice and Dice Recipes

Cornerstone: One Book

The word count for a typical paperback business book ranges from 40,000 to 50,000 words stretched over 10 to 15 chapters. That's a lot of content that can be sliced and diced into a variety of formats, lengths, and purposes. Here's a framework for how you could make that happen. And if your team doesn't have the time, you can outsource much of the content and editing work to companies like WriterAccess.

Here's what you can create from one book:

60 blog posts for your agency's website: Slice and dice each book chapter into five or six blog posts, then optimize that content for organic search. Post one new blog per week for the next 12 months, and you'll have all the content for your blog created, entirely in sync with the POV in your book.

60 videos for blog or YouTube: Take the 60 blog posts, slice them down into three or four talking points, and record a short three to four-minute video of you covering the highlights. Then post one new video per week on YouTube and embed the video inside the corresponding blog post on your website to further boost your SEO opportunity. And don't forget to optimize the title, description, keywords, and closed-captioning for the actual video on YouTube, too.

15-25 articles in owned media: Take the content of the blog posts or videos and combine, blend, and sort the content to create 15 to 25 articles you can pitch to the publications you know your target audience reads. Once the articles get published, you can share the links on all your social media channels. But be sure to put a list of where you've been published on your website, as well, with links to the actual articles.

60-email campaign: Take the 60 videos you recorded for YouTube and write a short intro, explaining how and why the video could be helpful to the recipient. Think of it as a helpful hint email series, and mail one weekly to your prospects and customers. As you get your articles published, you can mention those, as well, with a link in your emails.

60 videos for Facebook: Write a short-form post that summarizes three or four highlights for each of the videos you just recorded for YouTube. You could probably use the same copy as you used in the email series. Then post the short text when you upload the video directly to Facebook.

Note: Don't post the summary text and link to YouTube. Facebook doesn't want its audience leaving so they can consume your content on a different channel.

60 videos for LinkedIn: Rinse and repeat the same strategy for Facebook with LinkedIn. Upload each video directly into LinkedIn, for the same reason.

540 Facebook or LinkedIn posts and Tweets: Write one Facebook post for each of the three or four talking points identified earlier when creating the content for YouTube. Then scale that across the three to four talking points you would've determined for each of the 60 blog posts. At scale, you should now have content for approximately 180 Facebook posts, and you could likely reuse the content to post to LinkedIn and Twitter with minimal repurposing. And each of the posts will link back to the corresponding blog post on your website.

60 long-form LinkedIn posts: Summarize each of the 60 blog posts created earlier into 1,300 characters (not words) and post onto LinkedIn as a long-form "status update."

3 e-books: Consolidate the 60 blog posts into three main topics and stitch together the content into three short-form e-books measuring about 3,000 to 5,000 words each. Then offer the e-books for download off your website in exchange for an email address, or provide the content exclusively to your clients as part of your inner-circle strategy.

4 webinars: Take your book content and break it into four sections, then use that content to form the foundation of a curriculum you might teach during a quarterly webinar series. One could argue that your webinars may also be cornerstone pieces of content that could be sliced and diced into LinkedIn SlideShare files, social media posts, email campaigns, etc.

All totaled, you can likely slice and dice your book into at least 931 separate pieces of additional content that can be shared with customers and prospects in a channel-agnostic way.

Cornerstone: 52 Videos, a Weekly Series

Each of the weekly videos you record will most likely cover one central topic connected back to your POV in the form of a lesson, strategy, or tactic your audience can take for themselves and apply to their needs. You'll likely cover that one overarching topic by breaking it down into three or four talking points or sub-topics within the video. And if you do, there will be ample opportunities to slice and dice your videos.

Here's what you can create from a weekly video series:

52 blog posts: Once posted on YouTube, write a short paragraph setting up the video's content. Be sure to embed the YouTube video into the blog post, as well. You now have content for a weekly blog series designed to boost your site's organic traffic.

15-25 articles in owned media: Take the content of the blog posts or videos and combine, blend, and sort the content to create 15 to 25 articles that you can pitch to the publications you know your target audience reads. Once the articles get published, you can then share the link on all your social media channels. But be sure to put a list of where you've been published on your website, as well, with links to the actual articles.

60-email campaign: Take the 60 videos you recorded for YouTube and write a short intro, explaining how and why the video could be helpful to the recipient. Think of it as a helpful hint email series, and mail one weekly to your prospects and customers. As you get your articles published, you can mention those, as well, with a link in your emails.

52 video posts for Facebook and LinkedIn: Write a brief text summary or description of the highlights you covered in the video and upload the video directly into Facebook. Rinse and repeat the process for LinkedIn. You now have content for a weekly video series for both Facebook and LinkedIn with minimal repurposing.

540 Facebook or LinkedIn posts and Tweets: Write one Facebook post for each of the three or four talking points identified earlier when creating the content for YouTube. Then scale that across the three to four talking points you covered in each of your 52 videos. At scale, you should now have content for approximately 180 Facebook posts, and you could likely reuse the content post to LinkedIn and Twitter with minimal repurposing. And each of the posts will link back to the corresponding blog post on your website.

Cornerstone: 52 Audio Episodes, a Weekly Podcast

Each of the weekly podcasts you record, on your own or with a guest, will most likely cover one central topic connected back to your POV in the form of a lesson, strategy, or tactic your audience can take and apply. You'll likely cover that one overarching topic by breaking it down into three or four talking points or sub-topics within the podcast.

Here's what you can create from a weekly podcast series:

52 articles for owned media: If your podcast is 20 to 60 minutes in length, you could easily write an article from each episode to pitch to the publications you know your audience is consuming.

104 blog posts optimized for search on your website: Upload each of your weekly episodes to Temi.com and order transcripts. Then split the content of each episode into two blog posts for your website: 1) show notes which essentially highlights and promotes the lessons within the episode to encourage someone to download it and listen to it, and 2) a long-form post that shares the depth of two or three core lessons from the episode.

52-email campaign: Transform the show notes into a weekly email campaign and link to your website where subscribers can download the episode.

104 video clips for YouTube and social media: If you record your episodes with your guests using Zoom, experiment by turning your computer's camera on and encouraging your guest to do the same so you can record both audio and video. Then ask your team to select clips of the two best highlights and share them on Facebook, LinkedIn, Twitter, and YouTube, with links back to your website so visitors can download the full episode.

520 Tweets: Write 10 tweets for each episode highlighting one key nugget for listeners within each tweet.

156 Facebook posts: Each of your weekly episodes will likely provide two or three golden nuggets you could use in separate Facebook posts for your audience. Each episode of your podcast could provide you with enough content for a week's worth of posts depending on the social media calendar at your agency. Include a link back to the show notes on your website.

156 LinkedIn posts: Similar to Facebook, and don't forget to include that link back to the show notes on your website.

52 long-form LinkedIn posts: Take the long-form blog post you already created, cut it down to 1,300 characters (not words, but characters), and post it to your LinkedIn profile for each podcast episode.

156 Instagram quote graphics: Select two or three quotes from the content your guests shared during the interviews, or from your solocast episodes not featuring a guest, and convert them into a quote graphic, which is mostly text layered over an appropriately sized graphic for the branding of your show.

4 quarterly webinars: No matter which monetization strategy you decided to implement, having guests join you to share their insights and wisdom with your audience is an excellent strategy. That said, you should reserve every fourth or fifth episode for a solocast, just you and your audience exploring one particular topic with some real depth. We encourage you to approach your solocasts with some real intentionality because this is your opportunity to teach and share something significant with your audience. Consider this: what if at the beginning of each new year, you were to map out your 12 solocasts for the year in an editorial calendar and group the 12 topics into four categories, or buckets? Have the three episodes in each bucket transcribed, then blend the transcripts into a seamless webinar script. Your solocasts would, in essence, become the foundation for your teaching curriculum delivered via webinar to your niche.

4 lead-magnet pieces of content (or an e-book): Take the webinar script(s) you just created, along with portions of the slide deck from the webinars, and create a promotional e-book that can be used to build your distribution list with an email opt-in, or can be shared with your current clients as inner-circle content, or as part of the promotional strategy for the webinar.

1 book: The transcript from a 30 to 45-minute solocast is typically 3,000 to 4,000 words, which is very similar in length to a book chapter. Again, getting strategic about your 12 solocasts per year could give you ample content to write one new book per year if you were to use your solocasts as the cornerstone content to make it happen. And once your book is done, you can slice and dice the content using the steps found earlier in this chapter.

Cornerstone: 4 Keynote Speeches, One Per Quarter

Speaking can produce excellent cornerstone content that enhances your credibility. A key ingredient to being successful with speaking as your cornerstone content is to build out and deliver three to four solid keynotes, each including a depth of stories that are interconnected in a thought-provoking way to your POV.

Also, you'll be able to slice and dice more successfully and leverage each of your speaking engagements, especially if what you deliver has a bit of variation from speech to speech or if you invite Q&A at the end of the presentation. All of this can provide different content demonstrating how you interact with a live audience at an event, which can help you get booked more often, and provide valuable insights when shared with your agency's audience.

Here's what you can create from your keynote speeches:

1 book: Some professional speakers build their keynote speeches first, test the content with audiences, and if they feel there's traction with the audience, they'll blend three or four of their keynotes together and publish it as a book. Publishing a book leads to additional credibility, which leads to more speaking engagements. Be sure to take and apply the slicing and dicing framework outlined earlier for "Cornerstone: Book" as part of your content strategy. When you do, it'll be a strong example of how one piece of cornerstone content can spin off to create another big chunk of cornerstone content.

120 sound bite audio/video files: Always request permission from the meeting or event organizer to have a copy of the video recording of your session. If they're not planning to record your talk, ask permission to have someone on your team do it. In exchange, you'll provide the event planner with a copy. From each 60-minute keynote, you'll likely be able to select ten sound bites out of each of your monthly speeches, approximately 120 over 12 months. Ideal clips will be stories that engage your POV, stories related to the niche you serve, or the audience Q&A portion at the close of each keynote. The clips will serve as the foundation for social media posts, or as content to build out your YouTube channel, the blog on your website, etc.

120 video clips for YouTube: The video clips selected above will give you ample content to upload and promote at least two new clips per week for your channel subscribers. Be sure to optimize the title, description, and tags for each video you upload so you can benefit from the power of YouTube's organic search.

120 posts on Facebook: Each video clip you upload to YouTube should also be uploaded directly onto Facebook along with a short written description. Remember, Facebook won't give your video post much organic distribution if your post includes a link to YouTube. Facebook wants users to stay within its channel to consume your content, so providing native content will make that as easy as possible. And depending on your agency's social media calendar, you may be able to get several months' worth of mileage out of your 120 video clips.

120 posts on LinkedIn: Apply the same process you'd use for Facebook. You should also select the four or five best clips and link them to the "Professional Summary" section of your LinkedIn profile, so people who review your profile before connecting can get a feel for your content.

12 blog posts optimized for search on your website: Each of your speaking engagements will give you the opportunity to highlight something about the organization you were there to serve, something about the audience, any Aha! moments you witnessed from the audience, or some of the thought-provoking questions you were asked at the end of your speech. All of these can be blended and shared as an optimized blog post once a month. But it's important that the blog content doesn't make you the central character or the "hero" of the story. You're not. The audience is. That will make the content more enjoyable for your audience to read, more helpful, and you more likely to be invited to speak at other events. Michael Hauge's book, *Storytelling Made Easy: Persuade and Transform Your Audiences, Buyers, and Clients — Simply, Quickly, and Profitably* is a guide to doing this with excellence.

12 long-form posts on LinkedIn blogs: Take each of the blog posts you wrote for your website, slice and dice them down into 1,300 characters (not word count), and share them as long-form LinkedIn posts on your profile. Be sure to take advantage of hashtags, although hashtags within LinkedIn don't seem to have the same audience attraction power as on other platforms like Instagram.

12 articles for owned media: As we mentioned earlier, you can use the 120 video clips or the blog posts you created to write 15 to 25 articles you can pitch to the publications you know your target audience reads. Once the articles get published, you can then share the links on all your social media channels. Be sure to put a list of where you've been published on your website, as well, with links to the actual articles.

Other cornerstone content could include a regular blog or a research project. But by now, you've probably spotted the recurring patterns in the slicing and dicing strategy, which can be applied to these two forms of written content, as well, should you choose them.

Again, our goal with this section of the appendix was to provide you and your team with a usable framework and to illustrate some of the possibilities as low-hanging fruit. You should be able to apply the framework for all of your content no matter what form aligns best with your gifts and talents.

And we have no doubt you and your team have already created some ideas of your own on how to take some of the suggestions here even deeper into your niche. And that's awesome!

Appendix B:
Tools for Getting it Done

We're quite confident in the evergreen value of everything we've written, but here, when these lessons are put into practice, is where this plan all goes to pieces!

We know these tools will evolve, grow, go away, etc. At this moment in time (call it 2020), we believe these are some of the best options out there. Your mileage will vary, without a doubt. But this will get you started.

There are undoubtedly other tools out there. If you're already using tools different from the ones we've included here, and you're happy with them, then by all means, continue using them. But if you're looking for some new ideas, we hope you'll find this list a helpful place to start.

That said, the software and tools space is ever-changing. To help keep the list current, we created an online guide, what you might call a master list, at AgencyManagementInstitute.com/content-tools, where you can get the most up-to-date set of the tools our content teams are using.

We divided the tools into the following five categories:

1. Project Management and Scheduling

2. Audio/Video

3. Social Media

4. Monetization

5. Web/SEO

Project Management and Scheduling

- LastPass: a password management tool
- ScheduleOnce: guest-scheduling software that integrates easily with Zoom, Google, and InfusionSoft for monetization
- Zapier: integrations between different platforms

The goal with this suite of tools is to make it easy for guests to schedule time with you, reschedule, and receive reminders. We use ScheduleOnce instead of AppointmentCore (and we did extensive testing on both) because SO integrates so easily with Zoom, Google Calendar, and Infusionsoft (our customer-relationship management or CRM software). Seamless integration exists so you and your team don't have to complete these tasks manually.

When the system is set up correctly, you email your guests a link to your interview schedule, they click on the link and can access your calendar. They choose a day and time that you've pre-set to reflect your availability. They enter their information and submit the form, and the system adds the interview to your calendar and the guest's schedule with the necessary Zoom link for the interview, and the confirmation/reminder system is activated. No need for any personal back-and-forth communication.

You do nothing initially but write the follow-up email sequence and load it into ScheduleOnce, and you don't have to do anything else, ever! And in every email that the guests get from you is a link for different actions. If they have to reschedule, the program takes the event off your calendar and replaces it with a new one.

And all of that happens automatically.

Audio/Video

- Adobe Audition CC: used for editing multi-track sessions
- Amplify: raises or lowers the gain of the selected audio segment
- AnchorFM: records audio on the fly via your smartphone
- Deverberate: removes ambient sound in an audio track
- Fab Filter Pro G - Noise Gate: removes remaining noise floor after noise reduction is applied
- Grammarly: spell check and grammar correction for social media posts
- Libsyn: distribution and syndication of podcast episodes and data analysis
- Match Loudness: raises transient loudness to LUFS standards for podcasts on iTunes
- Noise Reduction: captures a virtual image of the frequency response of the noise floor, inverts the phase, then reapplies that noise floor to eliminate background noise like a computer fan

- PremiumBeats.com: finding and purchasing music
- QuickTime: playing audio at roughly 1.5 times speed when writing show notes
- Rev.com: quality transcription service priced at $1.00 per minute.
- Smart Podcast Player: customizable and easy-to-use audio player for websites
- Speech Volume Leveler: makes loud things quieter and quiet things louder and removes the overall dynamic range of the recording
- Speed - Time Warp and Adobe Audition: listen to podcasts sped up
- Temi.com: AI-based transcription service priced at 10 cents per minute
- Toggle Global Clip Stretching: listen/review to audio at three times the speed
- WriterAccess: a stable of freelance writers
- Zoom: records podcast interviews in dual channel audio, client meetings, and allows you to connect with team members
- Adobe Premiere Pro: industry-standard video editing software, used to create a timeline of the video for post-production editing

Sometimes we get audio levels from our episodes that are entirely messed up, so our team will need to reset volume levels. Amplify is one of the tools that does that. Deverberate also helps remove some of the echoing that could happen if you're recording audio in a room that doesn't have carpet. Deverberate is a plug-in that attaches to Adobe Audition and can solve the problem.

Libsyn is the web-hosting equivalent for a podcast. All of your MP3 files (your episodes) will live within Libsyn, which acts as the central hub that connects to iTunes, Google Play, Amazon Echo, Spotify,

Stitcher, and all of the other platforms through which you might share your episodes. Libsyn essentially takes your MP3 files and turns them into an RSS feed read by distribution channels like iTunes.

If you're building websites within WordPress, you're going to want to embed your audio files using Smart Podcast Player. It's about $100 per year and has become the standard audio player for offering visitors the opportunity to listen to your episodes directly on your website.

For show notes, WriterAccess has been a great resource. The content gets turned around quickly and generally runs $30 to $40 for a seasoned writer. We realize this may sound like ridiculous pricing, but we see the commoditization of creative work happening all around us. And the content is good. We see agencies working with WriterAccess and getting good quality blog posts for $60. WriterAccess can likely be an asset to your team, too. It's almost impossible to have even an agency employee do show notes for what it would take to assign the work to WriterAccess.

Social Media Tools

- Bitly: shortens links and tracks clicks
- Canva: creates quick social media images if needed ASAP
- Dlvr.it: will auto-share content to your social channels
- Hootsuite: schedules social media posts on Facebook, LinkedIn, and Twitter
- HotJar: monitors and helps you understand page engagement
- Social Oomph: creates a randomized library of tweets that get republished at scheduled intervals
- Tweetdeck: allows you to write tweets and check for character

counts on your phone

- Wavve: shares audio from your podcast, music, or recordings on social as video

What we like about Dlvr.it is that it shares certain blogs like MarketingProfs and others on a regular basis, automatically. You can set the product to go out to MarketingProfs, grab their most recent posts, and share them on your channels once a day, and you can tell it where you want it shared, specifically—Facebook, LinkedIn, Twitter, or anywhere else. And the comment Drew hears most often is, "You're on Twitter all the time!" And he'll say, "No, I'm not, actually. I'm hardly ever on Twitter live other than to respond when somebody is messaging me, but I'm tweeting all the time because I'm sharing everyone's content and opinions. I think you look less smart if all you do is share your own stuff. So I want to share other smart things other smart people are writing."

In Chapter Thirteen, we recommended writing 10 tweets (one for each nugget) out of your podcast episodes. You can take that library of content and load it into Social Oomph, which will randomize it and send a new Tweet from your library at whatever interval you set. For Onward Nation, we have a library now of thousands of tweets. Social Oomph sends a new one every 43 minutes.

Monetization Tools

- Clickfunnels: creates and deploys sales funnels amplifying your cornerstone content, conducts A/B testing, and integrates with a wide variety of tools
- EverWebinar: software for doing pre-recorded scheduled webinars
- Infusionsoft: CRM, automation, email, list-building

- HunterI/O: email list cleaning services

- Joinbytext.com: gathers phone numbers through an opt-in method

- Sublime Text: used for mass-HTML cleanup and provides the ability to edit multiple lines of code at once

- Zoom Webinar Extension: allows Facebook to broadcast podcast interviews as Facebook Live videos

Russell Brunson and his ClickFunnels team have built a robust platform including everything from sales funnels to webinar funnels, and their product integrates smoothly with Infusionsoft for all of our CRM work.

It was about three years ago that we did a deep dive into Infusionsoft because we knew we needed to pick a CRM. We evaluated many different platforms and options. Ultimately, we felt that Infusionsoft provided the most robust features for our budget as well as a marketplace of third-party apps that integrate seamlessly. The "Join By Text" feature is a great example. If you ever hear a podcast host say, "If you want that thing, just send a text to Six, Six, Eight, Six, Six." That's the Join By Text number.

Join By Text is also a great tool if you're a speaker. In every on-stage presentation, you should have something to offer via your Join By Text number. They get a text back that says, "Oh, you want the thing? Great." It gives them a link where they can go, and they can download whatever the thing was you decided to offer. Somewhere in that exchange, you also capture their email address, which is a great strategy to build your list, and you've also captured their mobile number. Then they're in your ecosphere at a couple of different points.

Web/SEO

- Ahrefs: helps with site audits, understanding backlinks, etc., for a particular site

- Answer the Public: shows the most common questions people ask about specific keywords and helps you find topic ideas

- Google Analytics: tracks site visitor data including A/B testing pages to deliver more effective content

- Google Keyword Planner: used for keyword research

- Google Trends: helps you identify what people are searching for and how frequently over a period of time

- Moz: valuable for a variety of different SEO tasks including keyword tracking, site monitoring, competitive analysis, and keyword research

- RavenTools: used for site audits and competitive analysis

- SEMRush: used similarly to Moz, can perform a variety of SEO tasks but mostly for keyword research and tracking

- SpyFu: used to "spy" on competitors' most profitable paid and organic keywords

- Yoast SEO: plug-in for WordPress, a must-have if you plan to do any SEO on your WordPress site

As we move into 2020, one of the most significant opportunities we see with cornerstone content is to not only map out the topics so they're helpful to your niche, but also so they sync up with search trends, especially those we see with Voice Search. We are taking a very strategic view of a guest list and making decisions about who to invite based on Trojan horse tactics, the expertise guests can share, and what organic keywords can be seeded into the show notes, blog posts, articles, etc., all of the downstream slicing and dicing that will drive organic search results and site traffic to your content channels. Yes, it will take you and your team some time to map that out correctly, but it's highly unlikely any other agency in your space will be applying the same level of strategic thought to their content creation.